SMP 11-16

Teacher's guide to
Book YX1

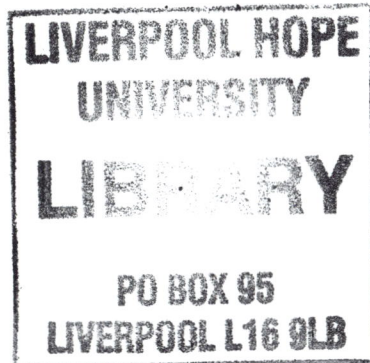
CAMBRIDGE
UNIVERSITY PRESS

Published by the Press Syndicate of the University of Cambridge
The Pitt Building, Trumpington Street, Cambridge CB2 1RP
40 West 20th Street, New York, NY 10011–4211, USA
10 Stamford Road, Oakleigh, Melbourne 3166, Australia

© Cambridge University Press 1995

First published 1995

Produced by Gecko Limited, Bicester, Oxon.
Cover designed by Gecko Limited

Printed in Great Britain by Scotprint Ltd., Musselburgh, Scotland

A catalogue record for this book is available from the British Library

ISBN 0 521 45744 0 paperback

Notice to teachers

Contents

The School Mathematics Project was founded in 1961 with the purpose of improving the teaching of mathematics in schools by the provision of new course materials. SMP authors are experienced teachers and each new venture is tested by schools in a draft version before publication.

Work on SMP 11–16 started in 1977 and the published version of the course started appearing in 1983. The original SMP 11–16 team was led by John Ling.

Since 1988, working groups have produced materials which have added to the original resource. This book is one of the results of this SMP 11–16 Revision. The SMP 11–16 Revision team, which produced this book, is led by Bob Hartman.

The following people helped at various stages in the writing of this book.

Graham Goodall   Mark Patmore
Bob Hartman   Eddie Wilde

Many thanks are also due to the following for their helpful comments: Colin Goldsmith, Liz Jackson, Rosemary Tennison and Nigel Webb. Others, too numerous to be mentioned individually, have provided valuable advice and help, including those at Cambridge University Press.

Since its inception, the SMP has always offered an 'after-sales service' for teachers using its materials. If you have any comments on SMP 11–16 or would like advice on its use please write to:

SMP Office
University of Southampton
Southampton
SO17 1BJ

Introduction to Book YX1

Starting assumptions

Book YX1 has been written principally for students in years 10 and 11 (S3 and S4 in Scotland). *Books YX1* and *YX2* will both be used primarily by more able students following the Yellow series.

Mode of use

It is not intended that *Book YX1* or *YX2* be regarded as texts to be worked through from cover to cover after students have completed *Book Y5*. They should be seen as a resource to be used alongside the Yellow series. Teachers will need to decide where the various pieces of content fit in with their own schemes of work.

It is not expected that there will be more than a few students using this text at any one time. With this in mind, 'Talking points' have become 'Thinking points' – many students may of necessity be working alone. However, this should be avoided as their sole mode of learning. (Some of the 'Mixed bag' problems are designed to encourage two or three students to work together.) This answer book has therefore been written primarily for students, but there are brief notes for the teacher at the beginning of each chapter.

The use of the computer and graphical calculators

It is highly desirable that students have access to one or more of these: a graphical calculator, a spreadsheet and a graphical device (also perhaps a programmable calculator or computer running BASIC). No attempt has been made to write material aimed at a particular calculator or spreadsheet. A conscious decision has been made not to refer to specific pieces of software as they are often superseded. Teachers are advised to look at publications such as *Micromath* and *Educational Computing*, and at up-to-date directories of published software such as that published by the NCET.

Equipment

Certain standard items of equipment are needed frequently and no special attention is drawn to them in the text. These include rulers, angle measurers, compasses and tracing paper. Occasionally reference is made to worksheets, and masters for these are included in this Guide.

A note to students

This guide contains fairly detailed working for many of the questions in *Book YX1*. These are designed to help you see where you might have gone wrong. They may show a method of solving a problem different from yours.

At various places there are extra questions in handwriting. These are meant to make you pause and think – you don't need to write anything down unless you really want to! If you disagree with any of these answers, after having re-worked the question, talk it through with a friend; if you still disagree, see your teacher.

Notes and answers for Book YX1

1 Angles and circles 1

This chapter concerns some of the more elementary circle properties, including angles in a semi-circle, angles subtended at the centre and circumference, and angles in the same segment. Previous contact with circle geometry may have been with circumference in *Book Y1* (Chapter 7, 'Polygons and circles'), or angle and area work in *Book Y2* (Chapter 13, 'Area'), *Book Y4* (Chapter 4, 'Angle relationships') and in *Book Y5* (Chapter 1, 'Surfaces'). Students are also introduced to the idea of deductive proof.

Section A begins with a locus problem. Some students may need reminding of the definition of a locus. Section B begins with a formal proof that the angle at the centre is twice the angle at the circumference. In the course of this chapter the following items of vocabulary will be encountered: special case, angle at the centre/circumference, proof, segment, chord, cyclic quadrilateral and deduction.

Most of the results from this chapter may be illustrated graphically with the aid of *Cabri-géomètre* (University of Grenoble, available from Chartwell-Bratt) or *The Geometer's Sketchpad* (Key Curriculum Press, available from Capedia). Nevertheless, it is crucial that students do not consider a particular result, however often it is observed, constitutes a proof. This should be brought out in discussion.

A Angle in a semi-circle

A1 The locus of point P is a semi-circle with the line AB as diameter.
Make sure you are convinced of this.

A2 The locus of point P is part of a circle, but for both these cases AB is not a diameter.
Don't forget the point P can be either side of the line AB.

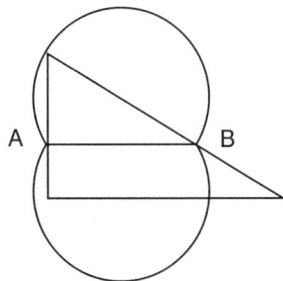

A3 The angle APB ($\angle$APB) is a right-angle.

A4 (a) They are radii.
(b) They are equal angles in an isosceles triangle.
(c) They are equal angles in an isosceles triangle.
(d) The sum of the angles in a triangle is 180°.

A5 *There may be several different ways to do these. Your working should be clear enough so that someone else can understand exactly what you have done.*
(a) $p = 90° - 55° = 35°$ (angle in a semi-circle)
$q = 35°$ ($\triangle$ABO is isosceles)
$r = 180° - (35° + 35°) = 110°$
    (angles of a triangle sum to 180°, or angles in a triangle)
(b) $x = 40°$ ($\triangle$BOC is isosceles)
$y = 180° - (40° + 40°)$ (angles in a triangle)
$\ = 100°$
$z = 80°$ (angles on a straight line)

(c) $s = 25°$ ($\triangle$BOC is isosceles)
$t = 180° - (25° + 25°)$ (angles in a triangle)
$\ = 130°$
$u = 50°$ (angles on a straight line)
$v = \dfrac{180° - 50°}{2} = 65°$ ($\triangle$BOA is isosceles)

A6 (a) $b = 20°$ ($\triangle$ADO is isosceles)
$c = 140°$ (angles of $\triangle$ABO)
$d = 40°$ (angles on a straight line)
(b) $b = 25°$ $c = 130°$ $d = 50°$
(c) $b = 30°$ $c = 120°$ $d = 60°$
(d) $b = 70°$ $c = 40°$ $d = 140°$
(e) $d = 2 \times a$

A7

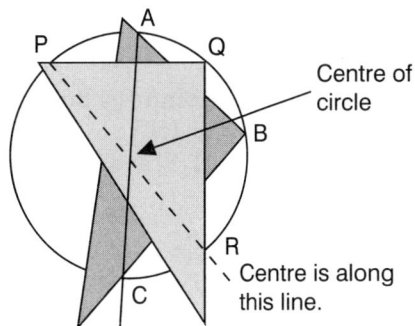

Use a set-square (or otherwise) to construct $\angle$B = 90° on the circumference. The points on the circumference cut by the set-square are A and C. Join AC – this is a diameter.
Repeat the process to draw another diameter. The corresponding diameter is PR.
Where the lines AC and PR cross is the centre of the circle.
Can you explain why your method works?

B Angles on the circumference

B1 Here is one possible proof.

$\angle OPA = \angle OAP$ ($\triangle AOP$ is isosceles)
$\angle OPB = \angle OBP$ ($\triangle BOP$ is isosceles)
So $\angle AOP = 180° - 2(\angle OPA)$ (angles in a triangle)
   $\angle BOP = 180° - 2(\angle OPB)$ (angles in a triangle)
So $\angle AOB = 360° - \angle AOP - \angle BOP$
   (angles round a point)
   $= 360° - 360° + 2(\angle OPA) + 2(\angle OPB)$
   $= 2(\angle APB)$

So the angle at the centre is twice the angle at the circumference.

Don't forget to give a reason for each step of your working.

B2 (a) $x = \dfrac{50°}{2} = 25°$ (angle at circumference is half angle at centre)

(b) $y = 2 \times 57° = 114°$ (angle at centre is twice angle at circumference)

(c) $s = \dfrac{110°}{2} = 55°$ (angle at circumference is half angle at centre)

$r = \dfrac{180° - 110°}{2} = 35°$ (equal angles in an isosceles triangle)

(d) $p = 180° - 2 \times 36°$ (equal angles in an isosceles triangle)
   $= 108°$

$q = \dfrac{108°}{2} = 54°$ (angle at circumference is half angle at centre)

(e) $u = \dfrac{162°}{2} = 81°$ (angle at circumference is half angle at centre)

$t = 180° - 81°$ (angles on a straight line)
   $= 99°$

(f) $z = 180° - 132°$ (angles on a straight line)
   $= 48°$

$w = 2 \times 48° = 96°$ (angle at centre is twice angle at circumference)

B3 (a) The circle is divided into 12 equal segments each making an angle at the centre of
$\dfrac{360°}{12} = 30°$.
The angle made at the centre by the chord from 4 to 9 is $5 \times 30° = 150°$.
So the angle between [1, 9] and [1, 4] is
$\dfrac{150°}{2} = 75°$.

(b) (i) $\dfrac{90°}{2} = 45°$ (ii) $\dfrac{60°}{2} = 30°$

(c) The angle between [a, b] and [a, c] is equal to half the size of the angle between the line going from b to the centre of the circle and the line from c to the centre.

B4 Both a and b are equal to half the angle at the centre O, so $a = b$.

B5 (a) $r = \dfrac{260°}{2} = 130°$ (angle at circumference is half angle at centre)

(b) $s = 2 \times 115° = 230°$ (angle at centre is twice angle at circumference)

$t = 360° - 230° = 130°$ (angles round a point sum to 360°)

(c) $u = 360° - 150° = 210°$ (angles round a point sum to 360°)

$v = \dfrac{210°}{2} = 105°$ (angle at circumference is half angle at centre)

(d) $w = 2 \times 52° = 104°$ (angle at centre is twice angle at circumference)

$x = 360° - 104° = 256°$ (angles round a point sum to 360°)

$z = \dfrac{256°}{2} = 128°$ (angle at circumference is half angle at centre)

B6

Statement	Reason
Let $\angle OPA = x$	
Let $\angle OPB = y$	
$\triangle POA$ is isoceles	*Sides OP and OA are radii of a circle*
$\angle OPA = \angle OAP$	*$\triangle POA$ is isosceles*
So $\angle POA = 180° - 2x$	*Angles in a triangle sum to 180°*
$\triangle POB$ is isosceles	*Sides OP and OB are radii of a circle*
$\angle OPB = \angle OBP$	*$\triangle POB$ is isosceles*
So $\angle POB = 180° - 2y$	*Angles in a triangle sum to 180°*
$\angle AOB = \angle POB - \angle POA$	
So $\angle AOB = (180° - 2y)$ $- (180° - 2x)$	
$\angle AOB = 2(x - y)$	
But $\angle APB = x - y$	
$\therefore \angle AOB = 2(\angle APB)$	

C Angles in the same segment

C1 The pairs of angles c and d are pairs of equal angles.

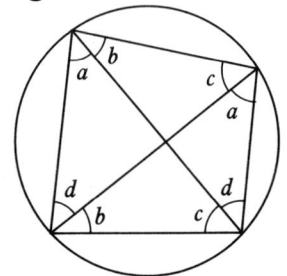

C2 $p = 180° - 100°$ (angles on a straight line
    $= 80°$ sum to 180°)
    $q = 180° - 65° - 80°$ (angles in a triangle
    $= 35°$ sum to 180°)
    $r = 35°$ (q and r are in same segment)
    $s = 65°$ (angles in same segment)

C3 (a) $r = s$ (angles in same segment)
        $= \dfrac{90°}{2}$ (angle at circumference is
               half angle at centre)
        $= 45°$

    (b) $u = 30°$ (angles in same segment)
        $t = 2 \times 30°$ (angle at centre is twice
        $= 60°$ angle at circumference)

    (c) $v = 180° - 2 \times 70°$ (angles in isosceles
        $= 40°$ triangle)
        $x = w = \dfrac{40°}{2}$ (angle at circumference is
                   half angle at centre)
          $= 20°$

    (d) $z = 30°$ (angles in same segment)
        $y = 180° - (90° + 30°)$ (angles in a triangle)
        $= 60°$

D   Cyclic quadrilaterals

D1 (a) $\angle BAD$ and $\angle BCD$ sum to 180°.
      $\angle ABC$ and $\angle CDA$ sum to 180°.
      *The sum of your measured angles may differ
      slightly from 180°.*
    (b) Opposite angles of cyclic quadrilaterals seem
      to sum to 180° **within experimental error.**

D2 (a) $\angle ACD = p$ because it is in the same segment
      as p.
    (b) $\angle DAC = q$ because it is in the same segment.
    (c) $\angle CAB = \angle CDB = r$
      $\angle ADB = \angle ACB = s$
    (d) In the triangle ABC the sum of the angles is 180°,
      so $r + p + q + s = 180°$.
    (e) The opposite angles of the quadrilateral are
      $(p + q)$ and $(r + s)$, which is a total of 180°.

D3 The quadrilateral is made
from four isosceles
triangles. Call these
triangles A, B, C and D.

Each of these triangles
has two equal angles.
Call each angle of these
pairs a, b, c and d. The
sum of the angles of
the quadrilateral
is $2a + 2b + 2c + 2d = 360°$.

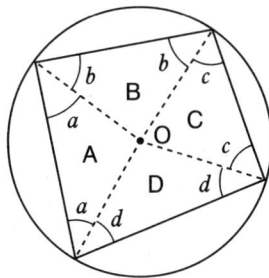

So $a + b + c + d = 180°$

But $a + b + c + d$ is the sum of the opposite
angles, so the result is proved.

D4 This diagram shows a
cyclic quadrilateral.
Two opposite angles in
the quadrilateral are a
and b.
The corresponding
angles at the centre of
the circle are $2a$ and $2b$.
The sum of $2a$ and $2b$
is 360° (one complete
turn is 360°). So the sum of a and b must be 180°.

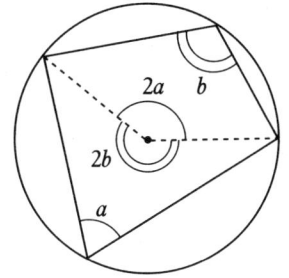

D5 *There is usually more than one way to solve problems
like these.*
    (a) $n = 360° - 2 \times 80° = 200°$
      $m = \dfrac{200°}{2} = 100°$
      or $m + 80° = 180°$ (opposite angles of a
                         cyclic quadrilateral)

    (b) $q = \dfrac{150°}{2} = 75°$ (angle at circumference is
                       half angle at centre)
      $p = 180° - 75° = 105°$ (opposite angles of a
                           cyclic quadrilateral)

    (c) Join DB.
      $\angle DBC = 90°$ (angle in a semi-circle)
      $\angle ABC = 110°$ (opposite angle of a cyclic
                        quadrilateral)
      so $\angle DBA = 110° - 90° = 20°$
      $\therefore r = 180° - 2 \times 20°$ (ΔDAB is isosceles)
          $= 140°$
    (d) $\angle DAB = 90°$ (angle in a semi-circle)
      $\angle ADB = 45°$ (ΔABD is isosceles)
      so $t = 45°$ (angles in the same segment)

D6 (a) This diagram is
not to scale.
As ABCD is a
parallelogram then
$\angle ADC = \angle ABC$.
But as ABCD is a
cyclic quadrilateral
these angles sum
to 180°.

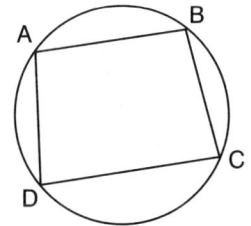

This means that both these angles are 90°.
The same is true for $\angle DAB$ and $\angle DCB$.
So a cyclic parallelogram must be a rectangle.

    (b) Here is a cyclic
trapezium; the sides AB
and DC are parallel. As
AB is parallel to DC then
$\angle BAD + \angle ADC = 180°$.
But as ABCD is a cyclic
quadrilateral,
$\angle BAD + \angle DCB = 180°$,
so $\angle ADC = \angle DCB$.
Similarly for $\angle DAB$ and $\angle ABC$.

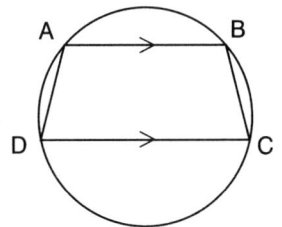

This means that the trapezium has a line of
symmetry passing through the centre of the
circle. (*Can you explain why?*)

D7 The sum of alternate interior angles is 360°. In this cyclic hexagon lines are drawn from each vertex to the centre O. Each side of the hexagon forms the base of an isosceles triangle.

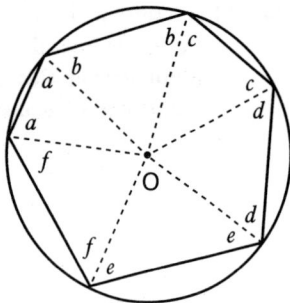

The equal pairs of angles are labelled a, b, c, d, e and f. The sum of the internal angles of a hexagon is 720°,

so $a + a + b + b + c + c + d + d + e + e + f + f$
$= 2(a + b + c + d + e + f) = 720°$

so $(a + b + c + d + e + f) = 360°$.

From the diagram, the sum of any three alternate angles is $a + b + c + d + e + f$ which is 360°.

D8 The quadrilaterals have these properties; you may have found others.

The line OB is always a line of symmetry.

$\angle BAO = \angle BCO$ (proved by using isosceles triangles)

If $\angle ABC = x$ then the opposite angle is $360° - 2x$, or opposite angles sum to $360° - x$.

Therefore the other angles are each $\frac{x}{2}$.

The two diagonals cut at right-angles.

These can all be easily proved.

E Deduction

E1 *Make sure that you always explain your reasons.*
(a) $a = 31°, b = 80°$ (b) $c = 54°, d = 34°, e = 34°$
(c) $f = 70°, g = 40°$ (d) $h = 55°, i = 155°$

The sketches in E2 and E3 are only rough; yours may be slightly different.

E2

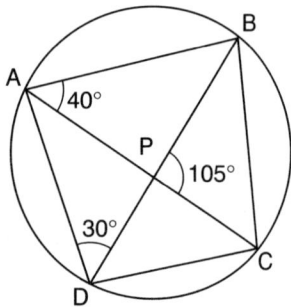

$\angle APB = 180° - 105°$ (angles on a line)
$\quad = 75°$
$\angle ABP = 180° - 40° - 75°$ (angles in a triangle)
$\quad = 65°$
$\angle DCP = \angle ABP = 65°$ (angles in same segment)
$\angle PCB = \angle ADP = 30°$ (angles in same segment)
$\angle BCD = \angle DCP + \angle PCB$
$\therefore \angle BCD = 65° + 30° = 95°$

E3

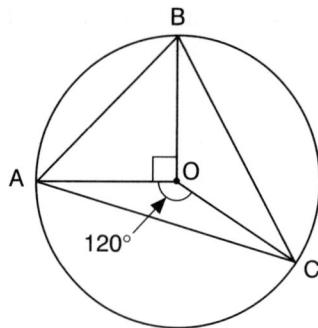

$\angle ACB = \frac{1}{2}\angle AOB = 45°$ (angle at circumference is half angle at centre)
$\angle ABC = \frac{1}{2}\angle AOC = 60°$ (angle at circumference is half angle at centre)
$\angle BAC = 180° - 60° - 45°$ (angles in a triangle)
$\quad = 75°$

E4 (a) The sum of the interior angles of a triangle is 180°.
(b) Angles on a straight line sum to 180°.
(c) $\angle ACB + \angle \mathbf{CBA} + \angle \mathbf{BAC} = 180°$
$\angle ACB + \angle \mathbf{BCD} = 180°$
$\therefore \angle \mathbf{CBA} + \angle \mathbf{BAC} = \angle \mathbf{BCD}$
(*Make sure you agree with this.*)

E5 The measures of the marked arcs are:
(a) 40° (angle at centre is twice angle at circumference)
(b) 220° (angle at centre is twice angle at circumference and angles at a point sum to 360°)
(c) 70° (alternate angles between parallel lines and angle at centre is twice angle at circumference)

E6 $\angle RSU = \angle SUT$ (alternate angles)
$\phi_A = 2 \times \angle RSU$
$\phi_B = 2 \times \angle SUT$
so $\phi_A = \phi_B$

Thinking point
$\angle PRQ = 90°$ (angle in a semi-circle)
$\angle SRQ = 90°$ (angle in a semi-circle)
so PRS must be a straight line.
Therefore PMNS cannot be a straight line as there can only be one straight line joining P and S.
Therefore M, R and N are the same point.

E7 As angles in the same segment are equal, then if the angle subtended by the arc BA is equal to $\angle ACB$ the point is on the circle. For a point outside the circle, the angle must be less than $\angle ACB$.

E8 (a)

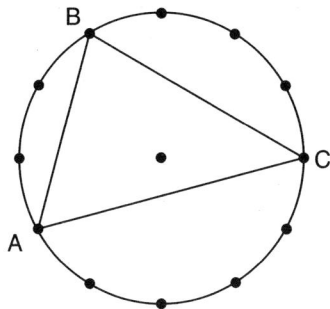

If $\angle ABC = 90°$ then AC must be a diameter; the centre spot is half-way along the side AC. If $\angle ABC$ is less than 90° then the centre spot is inside the triangle, but if it is greater than 90° it is outside the triangle.

(b) Your own observations

Here is a way of finding an expression for the angle between the chords.

Let the positions of the spots on the ends of the chord PR be p, r and on QS be q, s (in a way similar to a, b and c in **B3**), where $p < q < r < s$.

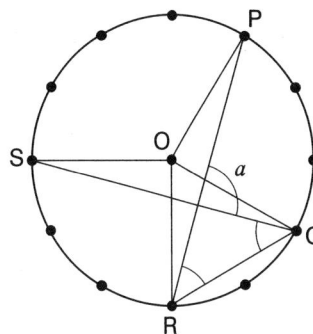

$\angle PRQ = \frac{1}{2}\angle POQ$ (angle at circumference is half angle at centre)

Similarly, $\angle RQS = \frac{1}{2}\angle ROS$

$a = \angle PRQ + \angle RQS$ (exterior angle of triangle)

$\therefore a = \frac{1}{2}(\angle POQ + \angle ROS)$

$\angle POQ = (q - p) \times 30°$

and $\angle ROS = (s - r) \times 30°$

Therefore $a = 15(q - p + s - r)$

Remember that there are two angles between the chords, which add up to 180°.

When the chords intersect outside the circle, the angle is given by $180° - 15(s + r - p - q)$. Prove this for yourself. Start by drawing another diagram, with chords PQ and RS where $p < q < r < s$.

(c) For 10 spots, $a = 18(q - p + s - r)$

Rooting around ...

This section gives students practice in manipulating expressions involving square roots. Some of these skills will be needed for the next chapter, 'Rational and irrational numbers'. Students need to be aware of the advantages of 'carrying round' a root in manipulations rather than reaching straight for the calculator (see 'Too soon to calculate ...').

Thinking point

$\sqrt{(a^2 + b^2)} = a + b$ is only true if a or b, or both, equals zero.

1 (a) $\dfrac{2}{\sqrt{3}} \times \dfrac{\sqrt{3}}{\sqrt{3}} = \dfrac{2\sqrt{3}}{3}$

  (b) $\dfrac{6}{\sqrt{2}} \times \dfrac{\sqrt{2}}{\sqrt{2}} = \dfrac{6\sqrt{2}}{2} = 3\sqrt{2}$

  (f) $\dfrac{6}{\sqrt{3}} \times \dfrac{\sqrt{3}}{\sqrt{3}} = \dfrac{6\sqrt{3}}{2} = 2\sqrt{3}$

So (b) is equivalent to (e), and (f) is equivalent to (d).

2 $\sqrt{8} \times \sqrt{3} = \sqrt{(8 \times 3)} = \sqrt{(4 \times 6)} = 2\sqrt{6}$
$\sqrt{12} = \sqrt{4} \times \sqrt{3} = 2\sqrt{3}$
$\sqrt{6} \times \sqrt{2} = \sqrt{12} = 2\sqrt{3}$
So (a), (c) and (f) are equal, and (b), (d) and (e) are equal.

3 (a) $\sqrt{200} = \sqrt{(100 \times 2)} = 10\sqrt{2} \approx 10 \times 1{\cdot}41 = 14{\cdot}1$
  (b) $\sqrt{8} = \sqrt{(4 \times 2)} = 2\sqrt{2} \approx 2 \times 1{\cdot}41 = 2{\cdot}82$

4 (a) $\sqrt{6} = \sqrt{2} \times \sqrt{3} \approx 1{\cdot}41 \times 1{\cdot}73 \approx 2{\cdot}44$
  (b) $\sqrt{14} = \sqrt{2} \times \sqrt{7} \approx 1{\cdot}41 \times 2{\cdot}65 \approx 3{\cdot}74$
  (c) $\sqrt{300} = \sqrt{3} \times \sqrt{100} = 10\sqrt{3} \approx 10 \times 1{\cdot}73 = 17{\cdot}3$
  (d) $\sqrt{7000} = \sqrt{5} \times \sqrt{2} \times \sqrt{100} \times \sqrt{7}$
                    $\approx 2{\cdot}24 \times 1{\cdot}41 \times 10 \times 2{\cdot}65$
                    $\approx 83{\cdot}7$

5 Any number can be expressed as a number between 1 and 100 times an even power of ten, so the square root can always be calculated.

Thinking point

Any number between 1 and 100 can be expressed as a product of prime numbers between 1 and 100, so the square root can always be calculated.
For example,
$\sqrt{76} = \sqrt{(2 \times 2 \times 19)} = \sqrt{2} \times \sqrt{2} \times \sqrt{19}$

6 (a) $(3 + \sqrt{3})(2 + \sqrt{2}) = 6 + 2\sqrt{3} + 3\sqrt{2} + \sqrt{6}$
  (b) $(\sqrt{5} - \sqrt{2})(\sqrt{5} - \sqrt{2}) = 5 - \sqrt{10} - \sqrt{10} + 2$
                           $= 7 - 2\sqrt{10}$

7 (a) $\sqrt{8} + \sqrt{2} = \sqrt{(4 \times 2)} + \sqrt{2} = 2\sqrt{2} + \sqrt{2}$
                 $= 3\sqrt{2} = \sqrt{(9 \times 2)} = \sqrt{18}$
  (b) $\sqrt{8} - \sqrt{2} = \sqrt{(4 \times 2)} - \sqrt{2} = 2\sqrt{2} - \sqrt{2} = \sqrt{2}$
  (c) $\sqrt{24} + \sqrt{12} = \sqrt{(4 \times 6)} + \sqrt{(4 \times 3)} = 2(\sqrt{6} + \sqrt{3})$

2 Rational and irrational numbers

Section A begins with the conversion of fractions into decimals using long division, which leads to recurring and terminating decimals; reference is made to the 'dot' convention of writing recurring decimals. Students are encouraged to use a spreadsheet or BASIC program to aid calculations with recurring decimals. A 'super' calculator (i.e. one which will handle a hundred or more significant figures) would be useful here (see for example 'Longsums' which is one of the programs on *Maths with a micro 1*, RLDU, Bishop Road, Bristol). In Section B students are given the standard method of converting recurring decimals to fractions.

The terms 'irrational' and 'rational' are introduced in Section C. Several proofs that $\sqrt{2}$ is irrational are given; it may be useful to read through these with a small group. As the proofs depend heavily on 'proof by contradiction', the exercise following this introduction may be useful.

Some teachers may prefer to give their own favourite proofs. However, the ones presented here, especially the two involving the last digits and the number of prime factors, have the advantages of being relatively clear and adaptable to other numbers. (The latter can even be adapted to consider cube roots if the last two digits of the numbers cubed are taken into consideration! This could form a challenge for very able students.)

Students are asked to prove the irrationality of some square roots by adapting one or other of the proofs in the text. The final thinking point encourages students to discover for themselves that [irrational] × [irrational] can sometimes give [rational], [rational] × [irrational] always gives [irrational], likewise with [rational] + [irrational]. These points could form the basis for a group discussion.

Begin with the practical challenge 'Can you draw a kite which is also a trapezium?' The point needs making here that merely because the students find it impossible does not *prove* it to be impossible. Here is a short proof based on contradiction.

ABCD is the kite with AD = AB = a and DC = BC = b.

Assume that ABCD is a trapezium with AD parallel to BC.

Drop a line from D to BC so that BE is equal to AD ($= a$). This means that ADEB is a parallelogram.

So that in triangle DEC:

$\quad$ DC = b $\quad$ EC = $(b-a)$ $\quad$ DE = a

So DE + EC = b.

But DC is also equal to b, which is impossible, so the original assumption must be wrong.

AD cannot be parallel to BC, so **ABCD cannot be a trapezium.**

As a challenge, students could be asked to prove by a similar method that in the quadrilateral ABCD if AB + BC = AD + DC then ABCD cannot be a trapezium.

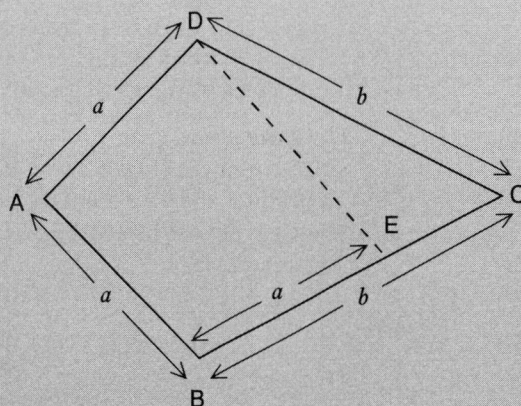

A Changing a fraction to a decimal

A1 To show that the block of numbers enclosed by the dots is repeated.

A2 The decimal of $\frac{2}{7}$ is recurring and so goes on for ever, so the calculator display must be less accurate.

A3 (a) $\frac{7}{11} = 0.\dot{6}\dot{3}$ $\quad$ (b) $\frac{4}{7} = 0.\dot{5}7142\dot{8}5$

A4 Two examples are $\frac{3}{8} = 0\cdot375$ (terminates),
$\frac{2}{3} = 0\cdot666\ldots$ (recurs).

If the only prime factors of the denominator are 2 and/or 5, then the decimal equivalent of the fraction will terminate; otherwise it will recur. For example, 1, 2, 4, 5, 8 and 10 all give terminating decimals.

Why not use a computer to experiment with some more numbers?

A5 Once a remainder is repeated, the sequence of divisions by the denominator is the same and so the decimal starts to recur.

A6 $\frac{1}{13} = 0\cdot0\dot{7}6\,923\,\dot{0}$ It does not have the maximum number of recurring figures.

A7 All decimal equivalents of fractions which 'go on for ever' eventually repeat. However some have a very large 'repeat unit'. For example, $\frac{1}{23}$ has 22 recurring digits and $\frac{1}{977}$ has 976!

When a 'remainder' repeats, the decimal must start repeating also. If you are not convinced, look back at the calculation for $\frac{1}{7}$ in the book, or run the spreadsheet program with some numbers of your own. The maximum length of the recurring block is one less than the number itself. *Why?*

Thinking point

Eddie is correct. The pattern of remainders will be the same as for working out $\frac{1}{17}$ because in each case you are dividing by 17.

Options

- (i) Numbers whose reciprocals are terminating decimals are:

  1, 2, 4, 5, 8, 10, 16, 20, 25, 32, 40, 50

- (ii) Numbers whose reciprocals have recurring decimals which recur in blocks of x digits:

Length of block (x)	Numbers
1	3, 6, 9, 12, 15, 18, 24, 30, 36, 45, 48
2	11, 22, 33, 44
3	27, 37
5	41
6	7, 13, 14, 21, 26, 28, 35, 39, 42
15	31
16	17, 34
18	19, 38
21	43
22	23, 46
28	29
42	49
46	47

The numbers less than 50 which give the maximum number of recurring figures (one less than themselves) are:

7   17   19   23   29   47

- With both sets of decimals the same digits occur in the same order but shifted in the recurring figures. For example,

  $\frac{1}{7} = 0\cdot\dot{1}4285\dot{7}$ $\frac{2}{7} = 0\cdot\dot{2}8571\dot{4}$ $\frac{3}{7} = 0\cdot\dot{4}2857\dot{1}$

  The digits 142857 are themselves interesting because $\frac{1}{142857} = 0\cdot\dot{0}0000\dot{7}$!

  With $\frac{1}{17}, \frac{2}{17}, \frac{3}{17}, \ldots$ these same digits occur: 0588235294117647.

  $\frac{1}{17} = 0\cdot\dot{0}58\,823\,529\,411\,764\,\dot{7}$

  $\frac{2}{17} = 0\cdot\dot{1}17\,647\,058\,823\,529\,\dot{4}$

  $\frac{3}{17} = 0\cdot\dot{1}76\,470\,588\,235\,294\,\dot{1}$ and so on.

Challenges

- How could you use a calculator rather than a computer to do these calculations?

- If you knew that $\frac{1}{17} = 0\cdot\dot{0}58\,823\,529\,411\,764\,\dot{7}$, how could you work out the rest just by multiplying?

B Changing decimals into fractions

B1 (a) $0\cdot85 = \frac{85}{100} = \frac{17}{20}$ (b) $0\cdot408 = \frac{408}{1000} = \frac{51}{125}$

(c) $0\cdot0256 = \frac{256}{10000} = \frac{16}{625}$ (d) $0\cdot0125 = \frac{125}{10000} = \frac{1}{80}$

B2 (a) $100 \times 0\cdot\dot{2}\dot{3} = 23\cdot232\,323\,232\,3\ldots$
$0\cdot\dot{2}\dot{3} = 0\cdot232\,323\,232\,3\ldots$
so $99 \times 0\cdot\dot{2}\dot{3} = 23$
or $0\cdot\dot{2}\dot{3} = \frac{23}{99}$

(b) $0\cdot\dot{5} = \frac{5}{9}$

(c) $1000 \times 0\cdot\dot{3}8\dot{4} = 384\cdot384\,384\,384\,384\ldots$
$0\cdot\dot{3}8\dot{4} = 0\cdot384\,384\,384\,384\ldots$
so $999 \times 0\cdot\dot{3}8\dot{4} = 384$
or $0\cdot\dot{3}8\dot{4} = \frac{384}{999}$

(d) $0\cdot\dot{4}\dot{5} = \frac{45}{99}$

(e) $0\cdot\dot{1}4\dot{8} = \frac{148}{999}$

Can you see a pattern?

B3 (a) Let $f = 0\cdot4\dot{7}$
$10f = 4\cdot7\dot{7}$
$9f = 4\cdot3$
$90f = 43$
$f = \frac{43}{90}$

(b) $0\cdot7\dot{2}\dot{1} = \frac{714}{990} = \frac{119}{165}$ *Start by multiplying by 100.*

(c) $0\cdot346\dot{1}\dot{5} = \frac{34581}{99900} = \frac{11527}{33300}$ *Start by multiplying by 1000.*

B4 Your own results and observations including: counting one- and two-digit numbers like 6 and 67 as 006 and 067, any one-, two- or three-digit number divided by 999 will give a recurring decimal whose repeat digits are the original number. For example, $\frac{7}{999} = 0\cdot\dot{0}0\dot{7}$, $\frac{17}{999} = 0\cdot\dot{0}1\dot{7}$, and $\frac{137}{999} = 0\cdot\dot{1}3\dot{7}$.

C   Irrational numbers

C1 $\frac{239}{169}, \frac{577}{408}$
$\frac{577}{408} = 1\cdot414\,215\,686\ldots$, which is $\sqrt{2}$ $(1\cdot414\,213\,562\ldots)$
correct to 4 d.p.

C2 For example, in the 3rd term $(\frac{7}{5})$:
numerator $= 7 = 3 + 4$ and
$3^2 + 4^2 = 5^2 = (\text{denominator})^2$
This only holds for odd terms.
Can you find a similar rule for the even terms?

C3 An integer must end in 0, 1, 2, ... or 9.
The last digit of any integer squared must therefore
be the last digit of 0^2, 1^2, 2^2, 3^2, ... or 9^2, so it can
only be a 0, 1, 4, 9, 6, 5, 6, 9, 4, 1 (1, 4, 5, 6 or 9).

C4 Your own proofs that $\sqrt{3}$, $\sqrt{7}$, $\sqrt{8}$ and $\sqrt{22}$ are
irrational. You may need to show them to your
teacher.

Challenge
Your own proof that the square root of any prime
number is irrational (probably based on the
number of prime factors).

C5 If a line passing through the origin has a rational
gradient it must pass through grid lines – the
gradient is the y-coordinate divided by the
x-coordinate of these points – a rational number.
(a) Yes, the line goes through (3, 2), (6, 4), ...
(b) Yes, the line goes through (2, 1), (4, 2), ...
(c) Yes, the line goes through (1, 2), (2, 4), ...
(d) No
(e) No

Thinking point
Wherever possible you should back these up with
examples. Remember that showing that a rule does
not work once disproves the rule, by definition!

- False. The product of two irrational numbers
  need not be irrational. For example, $\sqrt{2} \times \sqrt{2}$ is
  rational, but $\pi \times \pi$ or $\sqrt{3} \times \sqrt{2}$ are not.

- True. The diagonal of a square of side 1 unit is
  $\sqrt{2}$ units long – but can you draw a square of
  side exactly one unit?

- False. Squares of irrational numbers are not
  necessarily irrational, for example $(\sqrt{3})^2$ is
  rational but π^2 is irrational.

- False. The product of a whole number and an
  irrational number is always an irrational
  number. With a never-ending non-recurring
  decimal, no matter how many times you
  multiply it by a whole number the product will
  still be a never-ending non-recurring decimal.
  We can use this to show that, for example, $\sqrt{12}$
  is irrational, because $\sqrt{12} = \sqrt{4} \times \sqrt{3} = 2\sqrt{3}$ and
  we know that $\sqrt{3}$ is irrational.

- False. Adding together a rational and irrational
  number can never give a rational number, for a
  similar reason to that given above.

C6 (a) Let $\pi \approx 1 + \frac{1}{a}$, where a is an integer.

$(3\cdot1416 - 3)^{-1} = 7\cdot062\ldots$ $\therefore a = 7$
$\therefore \pi \approx 3 + \frac{1}{7} = \frac{22}{7}$

(b) Using $\pi = \frac{22}{7}$, area of circle $= \frac{22}{7} \times 7^2 = 154\,\text{m}^2$.
The answer is easy to calculate without the
use of a calculator. If $\pi = 3\cdot1416$ is used, then
the calculation is more complicated.

C7 $\sqrt{10} = 3\cdot16$ to 3 significant figures
$\sqrt{10} \approx 3 + \frac{1}{6} = \frac{19}{6}$

3 Tangents and curves

This chapter looks at the measurement and interpretation of gradients at points on curves. It begins with a brief review concerning gradients in general – including the common misconception that the gradient of a straight line can always be determined from the tangent of the angle the line makes with the horizontal. Gradients of curves are covered in SMP 16–19 in *Introductory calculus*, but the pace is probably too great for many of the students using *Book YX1*. Nevertheless Tasksheet 1, 'Zoom', may be found useful here. In Section 2.2, 'Obtaining a gradient', use is made of a gradient measurer; this could be introduced if appropriate. The datasheets from the SMP 16–19 *Teacher's Resource Pack* could be adapted.

In Section A the concept of an average rate of change in temperature–time curves is introduced. This is developed in Section B where the gradient at a point is encountered. Two approaches are adopted: first, the mean gradient of a straight line connecting two points on a curve as one point approaches the other; second, the gradient of the straight line at the point on the curve formed as a result of expanding the scale of the graph (or zooming in). The former, practical approach involves the use of a transparent ruler. The latter, generally speaking, requires the use of a graphical calculator or computer.

There are several good graph/function plotting programs available. One of the best is *Omnigraph* (Software Production Associates, Tewkesbury) available for RML Nimbus and IBM compatibles.

Section C involves students in measuring and interpreting gradients in various situations, including some consideration of the units of a particular gradient. Generally, students are asked to measure pre-drawn graphs rather than to spend too much time drawing their own. The difference between velocity and speed is touched upon in this section, although it is felt that some students will need help with this crucial point.

A Gradients and straight lines – a review

A1 Generally speaking, the gradient of a straight line is not simply the tangent of the angle the line makes with the horizontal. This is only true when the units on each axes are the same. Imagine how several different graphs of the same straight line look for different scales. The angle of the line will vary with each one, although the gradient must be the same.

A2 If two straight lines cut at right-angles the product of their gradients is $^-1$. For example, $y = 4x + 5$ has a gradient of 4 and cuts the straight line $y = \frac{-x}{4} + 7$ (gradient $^-\frac{1}{4}$) at right-angles.
If you are not convinced, draw some more straight lines with your graph-plotting device.

A3 $a = \frac{^-b}{c}$

The equation of the straight line is $y = \frac{^-bx}{c} + b$.

You may find it helpful to sketch a graph.

A4 The expression $\frac{y_2 - y_1}{x_2 - x_1}$ is valid for all values of x_1, x_2, y_1 and y_2.
(Don't forget gradients can be negative!)
Check these for yourself:

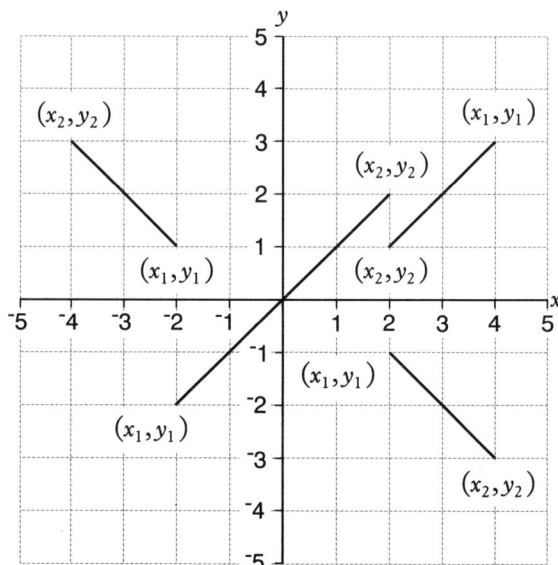

A5 The rate of change of y with respect to x on a straight line is the gradient of the straight line. If you are not convinced, look at the expression for the gradient between two points:

$$\frac{\text{change in } y}{\text{corresponding change in } x}$$

or the change in y **per unit change** in x.

A6 Your own graph with the lines AB, AC, AD and AE drawn on it.

(a) zero gradient: AD
positive gradient: AB, AE
negative gradient: AC

(b)

Line	AB	AC	AD	AE
Gradient	4	$-\frac{13}{12}$	0	$\frac{5}{3}$

A7 An important part of this question is the units.
(a) Heating up at a rate of $1\,°\text{C/second}$.
(b) Cooling down at a rate of $2\cdot5\,°\text{C/hour}$.
(c) Cooling down at a rate of $1\cdot5\,°\text{C/day}$.

A8 (a) Litres per minute – the bath is filling up.
(b) Litres per minute – the bath is emptying (a negative gradient) so as time goes on the volume gets less.
(c) Litres per pound – how many litres may be bought with £1.
(d) Kilometres per litre – distance travelled on a single litre (petrol consumption); this is given in car magazines to show how economical a particular car is.
(e) Pounds per kilometre – the cost of covering 1 km; this figure would be useful to budget for a journey. It might refer to the cost of hiring a car. (*Which costs the least per km: car, train or plane?*)
(f) Litres of petrol per kilometre

B The gradient of a curve

B1 The rate of change between $t = 1$ and
$t = 1\cdot5$ minutes is $\dfrac{40 - 34}{1\cdot5 - 1} = 12\,°\text{C}$ per minute
(or $12\,°\text{C/min}$, or $12\,°\text{C min}^{-1}$).

Using notation like $12\,°\text{C min}^{-1}$ is common in science, so litres per second can be written as litres s^{-1} or $1\,\text{s}^{-1}$, kg per cubic metre as kg m^{-3} and so on.

B2 $\dfrac{35 - 34}{1\cdot1 - 1\cdot0} = 10\,°\text{C}$ per minute $(10\,°\text{C min}^{-1})$

B3 (a) $2\cdot1\,°\text{C min}^{-1}$

(b) (i) $-4\cdot7\,°\text{C min}^{-1}$ (ii) $4\cdot3\,°\text{C min}^{-1}$
Your answers may differ slightly from these.

B4 (a) $0\cdot4\,\text{m h}^{-1}$ (b) $-0\cdot5\,\text{m h}^{-1}$

Options
Your own investigations of methods for finding the gradient of a curve at a point.

B5

x-coordinate	-2	-1	0	1	2
Gradient	-4	-2	0	2	4

You should have found that the gradient at a point is about double the value of x at that point.

B6 (a) The more you zoom in, the 'straighter' the curve appears. In frame 4 the curve seems to be almost a straight line.
(b) The gradient of the straight line at $x = 0\cdot5$ is a very good approximation to the gradient of $y = x^2$ at $x = 0\cdot5$, as the two lines appear parallel.
(c) You could draw the curve round $x = 1$ for $x = 0\cdot98$ to $x = 1\cdot02$. The curve is very nearly a straight line with a gradient of 2.

Options
- Your checks on **B5** using a graph-plotting device. Some graphical calculators are able to draw a tangent to a point on a curve.
- The gradient is equal to x^2.
  You may not have found this exactly because of experimental errors.

B7 Here are some values of x and $y\ (= x^3)$ close to $x = 2$.

x	$y\ (= x^3)$	Gradient
$1\cdot99$	$7\cdot880\,599$	$12\cdot0001$
$2\cdot01$	$8\cdot120\,601$	
$1\cdot999$	$7\cdot988\,005\,999$	$12\cdot000\,001$
$2\cdot001$	$8\cdot012\,006\,001$	
$1\cdot9999$	$7\cdot998\,800\,06$	$12\cdot000\,000\,01$
$2\cdot0001$	$8\cdot001\,200\,06$	

Your figures may not exactly agree with these because of rounding errors. From the table you can see that the gradient seems to be getting closer and closer in value to 12.

B8

x-coordinate	1	1·5	2	2·5
Gradient	2	3	4	5

The gradient for different values of x should be approximately equal to $2x$.

B9 Your own results and observations

C Using gradients

C1 (a) 400 metres/min
(b) The gradient of the line gives the speed of the shuttle.
(c) If the gradient is zero it means that the shuttle is not moving (it has zero speed).
(d) The completed distance–time graph should look like this.

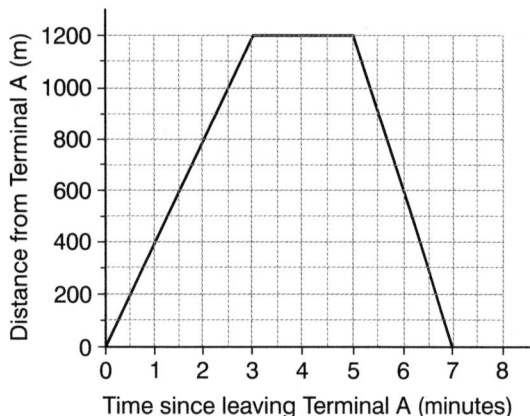

C2 The real distance–time graph would be more rounded. Nothing can change from travelling at 400 m/min to being stationary instantly (even if it were to hit something), so there cannot be sharp changes in gradient. The real graph would probably look like this.

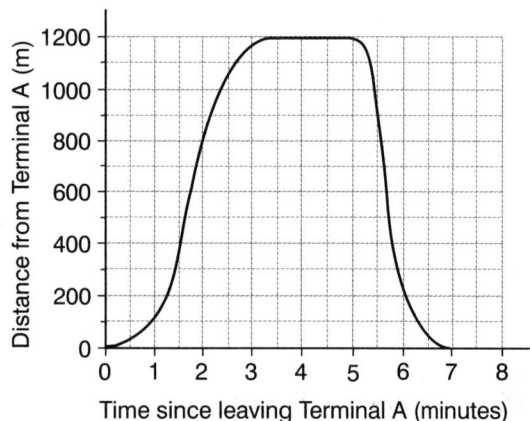

C3 The gradient of the learning curve starts with a zero value, increases slowly until it reaches a constant value which it stays at for a time. It then gradually decreases to zero.

C4 (a) (i) 100 m/s   (ii) 405 m/s   (iii) 320 m/s
Your answers may differ slightly from these.
(b) The rocket starts with zero velocity and increases until it reaches a constant value of approximately 1600 m/s after about 3·5 seconds. At 4 seconds after lift-off the velocity starts to decrease.

C5 (a) The acceleration is $\dfrac{80}{5} = 16$ km/h per second or 16 km h^{-1} s^{-1}. *Don't forget the units!*
(b) The acceleration is $\dfrac{160}{9\cdot8} = 16\cdot3$ km/h per second (to 1 d.p.).

C6 (a) Acceleration 2 seconds after lift-off ≈ 310 m/s^2
(b) Maximum acceleration ≈ 420 m/s^2

Thinking point

Generally, the path of the plane is completely independent of the shape of the graph showing how distance or velocity varies with time.
(Think of the velocity–time graph of a person on a roller-coaster.)

Too soon to calculate ...

This short section shows that in some circumstances it is advisable to carry expressions around without calculating their value until fairly late on. This is particularly so for square roots – in fact it requires less writing to carry the root around! There is also a little revision of the determination of the 'exact' values of some trigonometric functions.

The general theme of this section would benefit from being referred to on more than one occasion.

1 $OA = \sqrt{2}$ $OB = \sqrt{3}$ $OC = \sqrt{4}$ $OD = \sqrt{5}$ ...
It would not be as easy to see the pattern from the 'calculator' values:
1·414 213 562 1·732 050 808 2 2·236 067 977

2 $OA = \sqrt{1}$ $OB = \sqrt{5}$ $OC = \sqrt{14}$ $OD = \sqrt{30}$ ...
The iterative formula for t_{n+1} is $\sqrt{(t_n{}^2 + (n + 1)^2)}$ with $t_1 = 1$.
Can you find the position-to-term formula?

3 The 'exact' sequence is $\sqrt{3}$ $\sqrt{5}$ $\sqrt{7}$ ... $\sqrt{(2n + 1)}$.

4 (a) You can see why $\sin 60° = \dfrac{\sqrt{3}}{2}$ from the diagram on the left. The other sides of the triangles have been worked out using Pythagoras' rule.

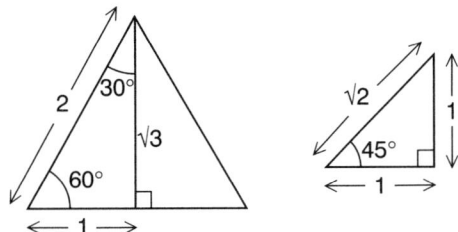

(b) and (c) Check your answers using this table.
It is useful to remember these exact values of the trigonometric functions.

Angle (a)	$\sin a$	$\cos a$	$\tan a$
30°	$\dfrac{1}{2}$	$\dfrac{\sqrt{3}}{2}$	$\dfrac{1}{\sqrt{3}}$
45°	$\dfrac{1}{\sqrt{2}}$	$\dfrac{1}{\sqrt{2}}$	1
60°	$\dfrac{\sqrt{3}}{2}$	$\dfrac{1}{2}$	$\sqrt{3}$

5 (a) $\dfrac{1}{2} \times \dfrac{1}{2} = \dfrac{1}{4}$ (b) $\left(\dfrac{1}{2}\right)^2 + \left(\dfrac{\sqrt{3}}{2}\right)^2 = \dfrac{1}{4} + \dfrac{3}{4} = 1$
(c) $\sqrt{2} \times \dfrac{1}{\sqrt{2}} = 1$ (d) $\dfrac{1}{\sqrt{2}} \times \dfrac{1}{\sqrt{2}} = \dfrac{1}{2}$

6 (a) $\angle EAB = 180° - \dfrac{360°}{5} = 108°$
$\angle OAB = \frac{1}{2}\angle EAB = 54°$
(b) Using the triangle OAY, where OA is the radius:
r (the radius) $= \dfrac{a}{2\cos 54°}$.
(c) Using the triangle ABX, $AX = a\cos 54°$.

7 (a) There are three possible positions for the point X which give different lengths of AX. Call these X', X'' and X'''.

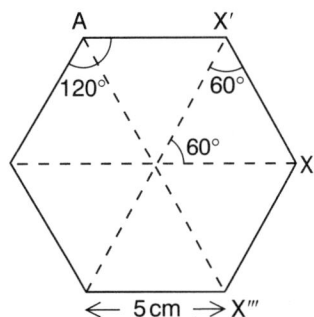

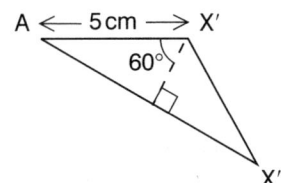

$AX' = 5\,\text{cm}$
$AX'' = 10\sin 60° = 5\sqrt{3}\,\text{cm}$
$AX''' = 10\,\text{cm}$
(b) Similarly, $BY' = d$
$BY'' = 2d\sin 60°$
$BY''' = 2d$

21

4 Compounding errors

This chapter is about how experimental uncertainty can affect figures derived from measurements. There are obvious links with other subjects, particularly Science, that involve measurement. It would be worth while to draw on the students' experiences of this.

In many respects, the work in this chapter builds on previous work in *Book Y2* (Chapter 2, 'Accuracy'). However, this is not an essential prerequisite providing students understand and are able to work with the '± notation'. It would also be useful if they appreciated that, unless stated to the contrary, measurements have an uncertainty of $\pm\frac{1}{2}$ unit in the last digit. It may be useful to comment on the possible uncertainty of figures quoted as, for example, 2300 metres. A short section relating to error and relative error may be found in SMP 16–19 *Mathematical methods* (Section 3.4).

The chapter begins with an experiment to find the velocity of light, suggested by Galileo in the 17th century, although there is some dispute as to whether it was ever performed. He had some inkling of human reaction times having an effect, so he suggested that the experiment be performed, 'after much practice', over two different distances, thereby eliminating reaction time considerations.

Section A is concerned with finding the maximum and minimum values of quantities given the uncertainty (given in ± form) of their constituent parts. Situations involving trigonometric situations are also considered.

In Section B the concept of relative error (uncertainty) is defined as a percentage. In Section D students consider the relative error arising from, for example, the sum or product of quantities that are themselves subject to a relative error. This treatment is informal, but some teachers may like to formalise this section to the extent of using quantities such as $(x \pm \delta x)$. This may be appropriate for very able students.

Section E shows students the necessity of sometimes considering relative uncertainties in terms of 'parts per million' rather than as percentages. There are obvious links here with Science, in discussing the accuracy in the determination of physical constants.

A   Measurement

Thinking point
What about the reaction times of the two experimenters? What time intervals would need to be measured for distances of a few miles if the speed of light is about 186 000 miles per second?

A1 (a) Maximum 64·5 °C   minimum 63·5 °C
(b) Maximum 30·45 m/s   minimum 30·35 m/s
(c) Maximum 1·505 volts   minimum 1·495 volts
Remember it is $\pm\frac{1}{2}$ in the last digit, which in this case is '0'.
(d) Maximum 2·055 seconds
minimum 2·045 seconds

A2 Giving the length as 207·3333 mm implies that the uncertainty of this measurement is ± 0·000 05 mm. This is clearly wrong. A figure of 207 mm, which implies an uncertainty of ± 0·5 mm, is more reasonable.

A3 Graham was probably wrong. Each individual cube may be anywhere in the range 3·5 g to 4·5 g.

It is very unlikely they would *all* be at one end or the other of this range. Therefore it would be reasonable to expect a proportionately smaller range of uncertainty for 1000 cubes.

A4 (a) 22 °C to 24 °C   (b) 112·25 m to 112·75 m
(c) 1·2 volts to 1·8 volts

A5 (a) (i) Maximum possible perimeter
= 18·5 + 15·5 + 18·5 + 15·5 = 68 metres
(ii) Minimum possible perimeter
= 17·5 + 14·5 + 17·5 + 14·5 = 64 metres
(b) Claire is right, as the perimeter is in the range 64 m to 68 m.

A6 The maximum total length of the two rods is
(2·5 + 0·01) + (4·2 + 0·02), which is
(2·5 + 4·2) + (0·01 + 0·02).
The minimum total length is (2·5 − 0·01) +
(4·2 − 0·02), which is (2·5 + 4·2) − (0·01 + 0·02).
So the total length can be written
(2·5 + 4·2) ± (0·01 + 0·02).
This shows that the uncertainty of the sum of the two measurements is the sum of the individual uncertainties.

A7 (a) A brick and its mortar are 75 ± 3 mm high. So for 100 layers, the height is $7 \cdot 5 \pm 0 \cdot 3$ m. The maximum height is $7 \cdot 8$ m and the minimum is $7 \cdot 2$ m.

(b) It is very unlikely that *all* the bricks and mortar in a single house would be at one extreme or the other.

A8 It may help to draw a line representing the ages of the items.

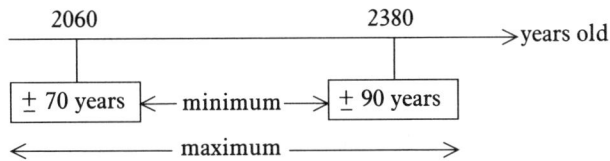

The greatest age difference would be $(2380 + 90) - (2060 - 70) = 480$ years. The smallest possible age difference is $(2380 - 90) - (2060 + 70) = 160$ years.

A9 Assuming that a is greater than b, the largest value of the difference is
$(w + x) - (y - z) = (w - y) + (x + z)$.
The smallest difference is
$(w - x) - (y + z) = (w - y) - (x + z)$.
So the difference can be written as $(w - y) \pm (x + z)$.
This shows that the uncertainty in the difference of two measurements is the *sum* of the individual uncertainties.

A10 Tariq has walked between 480 m and 520 m.
The distance between the two bridges is between 1150 m and 1250 m.
So he has to walk between 630 m and 770 m.
Or, from the previous question, the uncertainty must be $\pm (50 + 20)$ m, so the distance he has to walk is $(1200 - 500) \pm 70$ m or 700 ± 70 m.

Thinking point
Thomas is wrong because ± 1 m implies the measurement is to the nearest 2 m. He should have written $23 \pm 0 \cdot 5$ m.

A11 Lower bound
$= \frac{1}{2}(2 \cdot 5 \times 13 \cdot 5) + \frac{1}{2}(1 \cdot 5 \times 10 \cdot 5) + (10 \cdot 5 \times 13 \cdot 5)$
$= 166 \cdot 5$ m^2
Upper bound
$= \frac{1}{2}(3 \cdot 5 \times 14 \cdot 5) + \frac{1}{2}(2 \cdot 5 \times 11 \cdot 5) + (11 \cdot 5 \times 14 \cdot 5)$
$= 206 \cdot 5$ m^2

A12 (a) The measured depth is 20 m $\pm 5\%$ so it lies between 19 and 21 m.

(b) The boat C could be anywhere in the shaded region.

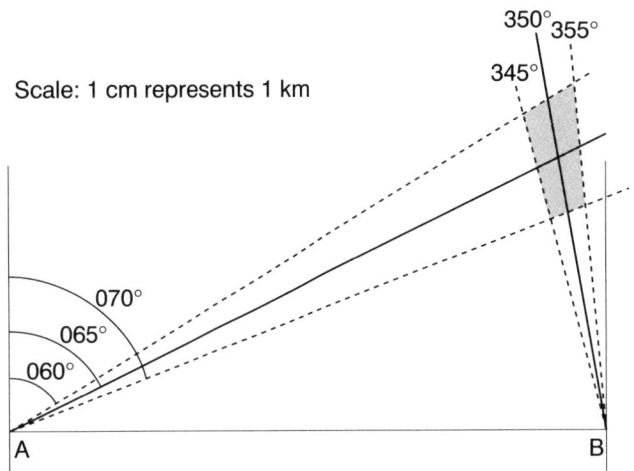

Scale: 1 cm represents 1 km

A13 Upper bound $= \dfrac{291 \cdot 5}{9 \cdot 8 \times 49} = 0 \cdot 61$ (to 2 s.f.)

Lower bound $= \dfrac{290 \cdot 5}{9 \cdot 8 \times 51} = 0 \cdot 58$ (to 2 s.f.)

A14 Maximum average speed $= \dfrac{100 \cdot 5}{14 \cdot 45} = 6 \cdot 96$ m/s (to 3 s.f.)

Minimum average speed $= \dfrac{99 \cdot 5}{14 \cdot 55} = 6 \cdot 84$ m/s (to 3 s.f.)

A15 In the range $0°$ to $90°$, increasing an angle increases the value of the sine of the angle (between $90°$ and $180°$).
What happens to the cosine of an angle?
Upper bound for $n = \dfrac{\sin 60 \cdot 5°}{\sin 42 \cdot 5°} = 1 \cdot 29$ (to 2 d.p.)

Lower bound for $n = \dfrac{\sin 59 \cdot 5°}{\sin 43 \cdot 5°} = 1 \cdot 25$ (to 2 d.p.)

A16 Between $90°$ and $180°$, increasing the angle gives a *decreasing* value of its sine.
Upper bound $= 0 \cdot 5 \times 10 \cdot 05 \times 10 \cdot 05 \times \sin 119°$
$= 44 \cdot 2$ cm^2 (to 1 d.p.)
Lower bound $= 0 \cdot 5 \times 9 \cdot 95 \times 9 \cdot 95 \times \sin 121°$
$= 42 \cdot 4$ cm^2 (to 1 d.p.)

A17 (a) In the range $0°$ to $90°$, the tangent of an angle increases with the size of the angle.
So maximum cloud height is
$42 \tan 5 \cdot 1° = 3 \cdot 7$ km (to 1 d.p.)
and the minimum height is
$38 \tan 4 \cdot 9° = 3 \cdot 3$ km (to 1 d.p.).

(b) For $d = 40$ km and $e = 5°$, direct distance to cloud $= 40 \cos 5° = 39 \cdot 8$ km. The difference between this and d is much less than the accuracy of the measurement of d, so it is reasonable to assume that the two distances are the same.

B Uncertain about uncertainty

Thinking point
Most people would say that 10 ± 0.3 volts was the more accurate measurement as it has the smaller proportional error: 0.3 out of 10 is smaller than 0.3 out of 1.

B1 *This type of question is a lot simpler if you use scale factors – to increase by 2% multiply by 1.02, to decrease by the same amount multiply by 0.98 to give the new value.*
All these answers are given to one decimal place.
(a) 44.1 mm to 45.9 mm　(b) $34.7\,°C$ to $35.4\,°C$
(c) 11.4 volts to 12.6 volts

B2 (a) 2 mm $\pm$ 25%　(b) 20 mm $\pm$ 2.5%
(c) 40 m/s $\pm$ 5%　(d) $85\,°C \pm$ 1.2%

B3 The side of the square is betweeen 98 cm and 102 cm, so its area is between $9604\,cm^2$ and $10\,404\,cm^2$. If there were no error the area would be $10\,000\,cm^2$. The lower value is $396\,cm^2$ lower than this and the upper value is $404\,cm^2$ greater. Both these figures give a relative error of 4% (to 1 s.f.). For fairly small errors, it does not matter if the relative error is calculated from the upper or lower bound. The relative error can be calculated from the mean of the upper and lower bounds but it very rarely makes any difference to the final figure for the relative error.

Thinking point
The area (see **B3**) is between $9604\,cm^2$ and $10\,404\,cm^2$. The problem (as in **B3**) is what to choose as the 'centre' value (sometimes called the nominal value) for the area. Is it $10\,000\,cm^2$ or $(9604 + 10\,404) \div 2 = 10\,004\,cm^2$? Providing the errors are not too large, it is simpler to choose $10\,000\,cm^2$ as the centre value and use a rounded mean value for the absolute error. For the case here it would be $(396 + 404) \div 2 = 400$, giving the area of the square as $10\,000 \pm 400\,cm^2$.

B4 Relative errors are easier to compare, so change the absolute error into a relative error.
1 km ± 1 cm is a relative error of ± 0.001%, which is better than the ± 0.01% of the other measurement.

C Worse and worse

C1 (a) The record speed was given in m.p.h., so the time of 15.56 s needs to be changed into hours. To do this divide by 60×60. A time of 15.56 s over the measured mile gives a speed of $\frac{3600}{15.56}$ m.p.h.
The time is given to 4 s.f. (a relative error of about 0.03%) so the speed should be given to a similar accuracy. According to the newspaper, the speed was correct to eight figures (a relative error of about 0.000 002%!).
(b) An uncertainty of 0.03% over a mile is $0.03 \times 0.01 \times 1760 \times 36$ inches, which is 19 inches to the nearest whole number of inches.

C2 The speedometer has a relative accuracy of $\pm$ 5% so the speed may be between 95 km/h and 105 km/h. The time to cover the measured mile lies between 59.94 s and 60.06 s.
The maximum distance travelled in 'one' minute is $105 \times \frac{60.06}{60 \times 60}$ km (the time in seconds needs to be changed into hours) $= 1.751\,75$ km, so a figure of 1.8 km would be reasonable. (*Why?*)
The new minimum distance travelled is $95 \times \frac{59.94}{60 \times 60} = 1.581\,75$ km ≈ 1.6 km.

C3 Some figures of your own supporting the statement

C4 (a) Assuming no uncertainties in any of the quantities, the heat loss is $5.7 \times 2 \times (16 - 14) = 22.8$ watts.
(b) Upper bound is $5.7 \times 2 \times (16.5 - 13.5)$ $= 34.2$ watts.
Lower bound is $5.7 \times 2 \times (15.5 - 14.5)$ $= 11.4$ watts.
(c) The heat loss is between 11.4 and 34.2 watts – a very wide range. This always happens when a quantity involves the difference of two others which are close in size and which both have an uncertainty in their values.

C5 Maximum dimensions: 2550 mm by 1275 mm
Minimum dimensions: 2450 mm by 1225 mm

C6 The size of the blanks can range from 399 mm by 159 mm to 401 mm by 161 mm.
(a) (i)　Maximum lengthways is 6 ($2550 \div 399$ rounded down).
(ii)　Maximum widthways is 8 ($1275 \div 159$ rounded down).
(iii)　So maximum number of blanks is $6 \times 8 = 48$.

(b) The minimum number of blanks is $6 \times 7 = 42$
($2450 \div 401$ rounded down by $1225 \div 161$ rounded down)

(c) (i) Maximum number of blanks $= 16 \times 3 = 48$
(ii) Minimum number of blanks $= 15 \times 3$
$= 45$

(d) Method B is the better way of cutting because at the very least you are able to get 45 blanks, as opposed to method A where the minimum number is 42 blanks.

C7 *Remember relative errors are usually only given to 1 (or occasionally 2) significant figures.*
(a) $\pm 10\%$ (b) $\pm 3\%$ (c) $\pm 10\%$ (d) $\pm 10\%$

C8 Scale factor $= \dfrac{\text{distance on image}}{\text{corresponding distance on object}}$
$= \dfrac{5 \pm 0 \cdot 1}{1 \pm 0 \cdot 1}$

So the upper and lower bounds for the scale factor are $4 \cdot 45$ and $5 \cdot 67$ to 2 s.f.

C9 Hamid's figures suggest that if two quantities have relative errors $a\%$ and $b\%$ the relative error in their product is $(a + b)\%$.

C10 Your own results suggesting that the rule breaks down when dealing with large relative errors. However, for relative errors of a few per cent it works quite well.

C11 Moira's guess is wrong. In fact for relative errors of a few per cent or smaller, the relative error when two quantities are divided is approximately equal to the sum of the individual relative errors.

Options

You should have produced your own figures and results to support your answers to these. A spreadsheet or small program might cut down on the number crunching and make it easier to do.
* No, the relative error is $x\%$.
* False, the relative error is $2x\%$.
* True

D The smaller the better!

D1 (a) Your own checks
(b) The rule does work for cases like $0 \cdot 93^2$, but they need to be written as
$(1 - 0 \cdot 07)^2 \approx 1 - 0 \cdot 14 = 0 \cdot 86$.
(The exact answer is $0 \cdot 8649$.)
(c) The approximation improves the smaller the value of x. For example:

x	$0 \cdot 1$	$0 \cdot 01$	$0 \cdot 001$	$0 \cdot 0001$
$(1 + x)^2 \approx 1 + 2x$	$1 \cdot 2$	$1 \cdot 02$	$1 \cdot 002$	$1 \cdot 0002$
$(1 + x)^2$ exact value	$1 \cdot 21$	$1 \cdot 0201$	$1 \cdot 002001$	$1 \cdot 00020001$

(d) This problem is easily solved using a spreadsheet.

	A	B	C	D
1	x	(1 + x)^2	1 + 2x	% difference (2 d.p.)
2	5	= (1 + A2)^2	= 1 + 2*A2	= (B2−C2)*100/B2
3	2	= (1 + A3)^2	= 1 + 2*A3	= (B3−C3)*100/B3
4	1	= (1 + A4)^2	= 1 + 2*A4	= (B4−C4)*100/B4
5	0.5	= (1 + A5)^2	= 1 + 2*A5	= (B5−C5)*100/B5
6	0.1	= (1 + A6)^2	= 1 + 2*A6	= (B6−C6)*100/B6

In fact, to be 'very small' x need only be about $0 \cdot 1$. The approximation $(1 + x)^2 \approx 1 + 2x$ can be very useful, for example
$101 = 100(1 + 0 \cdot 01)$, so
$101^2 \approx 10\,000(1 + 0 \cdot 02) = 10\,200$.
This approximation is a special case of the more general one: $(1 + x)^n \approx 1 + nx$.
So $(1 + 0 \cdot 03)^{\frac{1}{2}}$ or $\sqrt{(1 + 0 \cdot 03)} \approx 1 + \dfrac{0 \cdot 03}{2}$
$= 1 \cdot 015$ (by calculator it is $1 \cdot 014\,889\,157$)

D2 Here is an example of a spreadsheet showing how good an approximation it is to use the relative uncertainty of a quantity squared as $2a\%$, where $a\%$ is the relative uncertainty in the quantity.

	1	2	3	4
A	Quantity	Rel. error (a%)	Rel. error in (quantity)^2 (%)	2 x rel. error (a%)
B	100	1	2.01	2
C	100	2	4.04	4
D	100	4	8.16	8
E	100	6	12.36	12
F	100	8	16.64	16
G	100	10	21	20
H	100	12	25.44	24
I	100	14	29.96	28
J	100	16	34.56	32

For values a of a few per cent the approximation is good.

E Super accuracy

E1 1% is equivalent to $10\,000$ ppm, so $0 \cdot 01\%$ is equivalent to 100 ppm.

E2 5 cm in $380\,000$ km is an uncertainty of
$\dfrac{5}{100 \times 1000 \times 380\,000} \approx 0 \cdot 000\,13$ ppm!

E3 Uncertainty $= \dfrac{0 \cdot 11}{299\,792 \cdot 56} \approx 0 \cdot 4$ ppm

E4 Parts per billion $(1\,000\,000\,000)$ (ppb) could be used. The distance to the moon can be measured to an accuracy of $0 \cdot 13$ ppb.

5 Using graphs to solve equations

This chapter looks at solving polynomial and trigonometric equations by graphical means. It builds on work relating to the solution of quadratic equations in *Book Y4* (Chapter 17, 'Quadratic functions and equations'). Some form of graph-plotting device, calculator or software, is essential for this chapter.

Section A takes a brief historical look at the solution of both linear and quadratic equations, giving students the opportunity to perform some algebraic manipulations. A simple formula for the solution of quadratic equations is given and attention drawn to the fact that a square root has a negative as well as a positive value. In Section B, students are made aware that not all equations are easily solved using algebraic methods and that graphical methods could offer a solution. Students' attention is drawn to the fact that angles may be measured in radians as well as degrees – some may already be aware of this from their spreadsheet or programming experiences. Students are encouraged to use the zoom facility of their graph-plotting device.

In Section C, a conscious decision has been made not to specify the number of significant figures or places of decimals required in the answer. In some cases the question context should suggest a suitable accuracy, although in context-free questions some students may need guidance. However, the general topic is worth discussing.

A Times past

A1 (a) Let the two trial values be 1 and 3 (any two numbers will do).
These give false values of 12 and 20, so
$$x = \frac{12 \times 3 - 20 \times 1}{12 - 20} = {}^-2$$

(b) Let the trial values be 2 and 4.
The false values are $^-14$ and $^-18$, so
$$x = \frac{{}^-14 \times 4 - {}^-18 \times 2}{{}^-14 - {}^-18} = {}^-5$$

(c) $x = 3$

A2 For the equation $ax + b = 0$:
if g_1 and f_1 are the first guess and false value, then $ag_1 + b = f_1$,
and if g_2 and f_2 are the second guess and second false value, then $ag_2 + b = f_2$.

From these two equations,
$a(g_1 - g_2) = f_1 - f_2$ and $b(g_1 - g_2) = f_2 g_1 - f_1 g_2$

so $a = \dfrac{f_1 - f_2}{g_1 - g_2}$ and $b = \dfrac{f_2 g_1 - f_1 g_2}{g_1 - g_2}$.

From the original equation, $x = \dfrac{{}^-b}{a}$.

Substituting for a and b gives
$$x = -\frac{f_2 g_1 - f_1 g_2}{g_1 - g_2} \times \frac{g_1 - g_2}{f_1 - f_2}$$
$$= \frac{f_1 g_2 - f_2 g_1}{f_1 - f_2}.$$

Although this method may seem very cumbersome it had the advantage that once someone had learnt the rules they could solve any equation of this form.

A3 (a) If $ax + b = c$, then $x = \dfrac{c - b}{a}$.

(b) (i) $x = \dfrac{123 \cdot 5 - 1 \cdot 7}{6 \cdot 5} = 18 \cdot 7$ (to 1 d.p.)

(ii) $x = \dfrac{21 \cdot 74 + 3 \cdot 76}{1 \cdot 97} = 12 \cdot 9$ (to 1 d.p.)

(iii) $x = \dfrac{67 \cdot 21 - 7 \cdot 21}{{}^-3 \cdot 1} = {}^-19 \cdot 4$ (to 1 d.p.)

(iv) $x = \dfrac{{}^-56 \cdot 21 + 6 \cdot 7}{{}^-8 \cdot 1} = 6 \cdot 1$ (to 1 d.p.)

(c) Your own checks

A4 (a) $x^2 + 7x + 10 = 0$
$(x + 2)(x + 5) = 0$
So either $x + 2 = 0$ or $x + 5 = 0$
So either $x = {}^-2$ or $x = {}^-5$

(b) $x^2 + x - 20 = 0$
$(x - 4)(x + 5) = 0$
So either $x - 4 = 0$ or $x + 5 = 0$
So either $x = 4$ or $x = {}^-5$

(c) $x^2 - 4x - 21 = 0$
$(x - 7)(x + 3) = 0$
So either $x - 7 = 0$ or $x + 3 = 0$
So either $x = 7$ or $x = {}^-3$

A5 (a) $x = {}^-\frac{1}{2} \times 7 + \sqrt{(\frac{1}{4} \times 49 - 10)}$

$= {}^-\frac{7}{2} + \sqrt{\left(\dfrac{49 - 40}{4}\right)}$ (*Make sure you understand this step.*)

$= {}^-\frac{7}{2} + \sqrt{\frac{9}{4}}$

$= {}^-\frac{7}{2} + \frac{3}{2}$ ($\sqrt{\frac{9}{4}} = \frac{3}{2}$)

$= {}^-2$ (one of the solutions found in **A4**(a))

(b) $x = \frac{-1}{2} + \surd(\frac{1}{4} + 20)$

$\quad = \frac{-1}{2} + \sqrt{\left(\dfrac{1 + 80}{4}\right)}$

$\quad = \frac{-1}{2} + \surd\frac{81}{4}$

$\quad = \frac{-1}{2} + \frac{9}{2}$

$\quad = 4$

(When finding the square roots of fractions like these it is helpful to add the fractions together – the square root is then more obvious.)

(c) $x = \frac{-1}{2} \times {}^-4 + \surd(\frac{16}{4} + 21)$

$\quad = 2 + \surd 25$

$\quad = 7$

The formula only seems to give one of the solutions or roots.

Thinking point

The second root may be found by taking into account the negative value of the square root. For example, in **A5**(a):

$x = \frac{-1}{2} \times 7 + \surd\frac{9}{4}$.

This means that $x = \frac{-1}{2} \times 7 + \surd\frac{9}{4}$ *or*
$x = \frac{-1}{2} \times 7 - \surd\frac{9}{4}$.

So the solutions are $x = {}^-3 \cdot 5 + 1 \cdot 5 = {}^-2$ and
$x = {}^-3 \cdot 5 - 1 \cdot 5 = {}^-5$, which are the two solutions found by factorising in **A4**.

*Find the 'second solutions' in **A5**(b) and (c).*

A6 Using the formula $x = \frac{-1}{2}b \pm \surd(\frac{1}{4}b^2 - c)$, the '$\pm$' has nothing to do with errors! In this case it tells us to take into account both the positive and negative values of the square root.

(a) $x = {}^-2 \pm \surd(\frac{16}{4} - 10) = {}^-2 \pm \surd 14$

So $x = 1 \cdot 742$ or $x = {}^-5 \cdot 742$ (to 3 d.p.)

(b) $x = 1 \pm \surd(1 + 3) = 1 \pm \surd 4$

So $x = 3$ or $x = {}^-1$

(c) $x = 0 \cdot 5 \pm \surd(0 \cdot 25 + 10) = 0 \cdot 5 \pm \surd 10 \cdot 25$

So $x = 3 \cdot 702$ or $x = {}^-2 \cdot 702$ (to 3 d.p.)

Challenge

When the two roots are decimals, what do you notice about their difference and sum? You might find a simple spreadsheet or BASIC program useful. Do all quadratic equations have solutions?

B   When algebra fails!

Challenge

When you try to factorise the expression
$x^3 + 2x^2 - 19x - 20 = 0$ you will probably need several attempts!

$(x + 1)(x^2 + x - 20) = 0$

$(x + 1)(x + 5)(x - 4) = 0$

So the solutions are $x = {}^-1, {}^-5$ and 4.

Looking at the original equation $x^2 - x - 6 = 0$,
$x^2 - x = 6$, $x^2 = x + 6$, $x^2 - 6 = x$ are all simply rearrangements of the original equation.

B1 (a) $y = x^2 - x - 2$, B $\quad y = {}^-x - 1$, A
$\quad y = 2$, C $\qquad\quad y = {}^-3$, D

(b) (i) $y = x^2 - x - 2$ has the value zero at $x = {}^-1$ and at $x = 2$.

(ii) The solutions are the values of x where $y = x^2 - x - 2$ has the value zero, i.e. at $x = {}^-1$ and $x = 2$. *Why?*

B2 (a) The solutions are where the two graphs intersect, i.e. at $x = {}^-1$ and $x = 1$.

(b) The answers will give the solution to the equation ${}^-x - 1 = x^2 - x - 2$ because the graphs cross where both expressions are equal in value.

B3 The solution can be found from the x-coordinate of the intersection of $y = x^2 - x - 2$ and $y = 2$. The two solutions, to 1 d.p., are ${}^-1 \cdot 6$ and $2 \cdot 6$.

B4 The two equations are rearrangements of each other.

B5 The equation $x^2 - x - 2 = {}^-3$ does not have a solution because $y = x^2 - x - 2$ and $y = {}^-3$ do not intersect.

B6 (a) $x = 0 \cdot 5$ and $x = {}^-1 \cdot 0$

(b) $x = 1 \cdot 3$ *Why is there only one root to equations like $x^3 = a$?*

(c) $x = 0 \cdot 6$ and $x = {}^-0 \cdot 8$ (where the two curves cross)

B7 (a) $x = {}^-1, x = 0$ and $x = 1$

(b) $x = 0 \cdot 7$ and $x = {}^-0 \cdot 7$ (c) $x = {}^-0 \cdot 5$ and $x = 0$

B8 You need to extend the graph to the right. The third root is $x = 2$.

B9

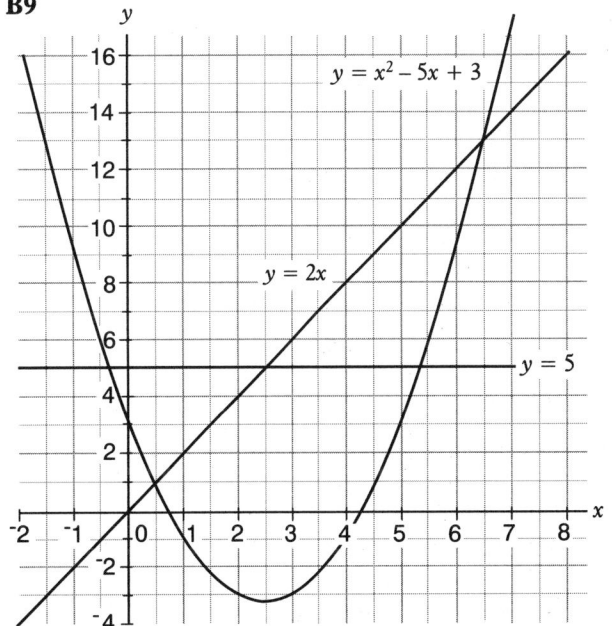

(a) The roots are values of x where the graph cuts the x-axis. The roots are $4 \cdot 3$ and $0 \cdot 7$ (to 1 d.p.).

(b) The roots are the values of x where the curve cuts the straight line $y = 5$. The roots are $5 \cdot 4$ and ${}^-0 \cdot 4$ (to 1 d.p.).

(c) The roots are the values of x where the curve cuts the straight line $y = 2x$. The roots are $6 \cdot 5$ and $0 \cdot 5$ (to 1 d.p.).

(d) First the equation has to be rearranged to make use of the graph $y = x^2 - 5x + 3$. Rearrange the original equation as $x^2 - 5x + 3 = 2x$. The roots of this equation are those found in (c). The roots are $6 \cdot 5$ and $0 \cdot 5$ (to 1 d.p.).

B10 To solve the equation $x^3 + x^2 - 15x = 10$, find the x-coordinates at the intersection of:

$y = x^3 + x^2 - 15x$ and $y = 10$

$y = x^3 + x^2 - 15x - 10$ and $y = 0$ (the x-axis)

$y = x^3 + x^2$ and $y = 15x + 10$

$y = x^3$ and $y = -x^2 + 15x + 10$

You may have found some more of your own. These all give the same solutions of $^-4 \cdot 1$, $^-0 \cdot 7$ and $3 \cdot 7$ (to 1 d.p.).

B11 The roots of the equation $2x^2 + 3x - 10 = 0$ are $1 \cdot 61$ and $^-3 \cdot 11$ (to 2 d.p.).

B12 The equation $x^3 + 2x^2 + 10x = 20$ has one root, which is $1 \cdot 4$, to 1 decimal place.

Thinking point

The equation $5 \sin x = 3$ could be solved by plotting $y = 5 \sin x$ and $y = 3$; the x-coordinate of the point(s) of intersection will give the solution(s).

With $100 \sin x = 50 - x$, $y = 100 \sin x$ and $y = 50 - x$ could be plotted.

Thinking point

In each case, ϕ is equal to $\dfrac{360°}{2\pi} \approx 57°$.

B13 (a) (i) $\dfrac{\pi}{2} = 1 \cdot 571$ (ii) $\dfrac{3\pi}{2} = 4 \cdot 712$

(iii) $\dfrac{\pi}{3} = 1 \cdot 047$ (iv) $\dfrac{\pi}{4} = 0 \cdot 785$

(v) $\dfrac{7\pi}{18} = 1 \cdot 222$ (vi) $\dfrac{151\pi}{180} = 2 \cdot 635$

(b) (i) $30°$ (ii) $135°$

(iii) $120°$ (iv) $286 \cdot 5°$

(v) $114 \cdot 6°$ (vi) $95 \cdot 1°$

In B14 and B15 you may have found it useful to change your calculator to work in radians.

B14 (a) $0 \cdot 5$ (b) $0 \cdot 866$ (to 3 d.p.)

(c) 1 (d) 1

(e) $1 \cdot 557$ (to 3 d.p.) (f) $0 \cdot 050$ (to 3 d.p.)

B15 All these angles are in radians.

(a) $\dfrac{\pi}{3}$ (b) $\dfrac{\pi}{2}$

(c) $0 \cdot 463$ (to 3 d.p.) (d) $1 \cdot 266$ (to 3 d.p.)

B16 (a) $x = 0 \cdot 8$ and $x = 3 \cdot 9$ (b) $x = 0 \cdot 4$ and $x = 4 \cdot 3$

(c) $x = 1 \cdot 0$ and $x = 3 \cdot 2$ (d) $x = 0 \cdot 4$ and $x = 4 \cdot 3$

B17 *Did you remember to set your graph-plotter to radians?*

Two solutions are $^-3 \cdot 21^c$ and $3 \cdot 08^c$.

It is usually easier to read off the values where a line or curve cuts the x-axis. To do this you need to rearrange the equation into the form f(x) = 0, *in this case*

f(x) $= 100 \cos \dfrac{x}{2} - x$.

B18 The two solutions are $^-0 \cdot 82^c$ and $0 \cdot 82^c$.

Thinking point

Two solutions to $\cos x - x^2 = 0$ are $^-1 \cdot 0°$ and $1 \cdot 0°$ (to 1 d.p.). As $1°$ is about $0 \cdot 017$ radians, there are different solutions to $\cos x - x^2 = 0$, depending on whether the angles are measured in degrees or radians (see **B18**).

Options

- When the angle x is measured in radians, $\sin x \approx x$ and $\cos x \approx 1$ for small angles.

- Area of sector

$$= \frac{\phi}{\text{complete revolution}} \times \pi r^2$$

$$= \frac{\phi}{2\pi} \times \pi r^2$$

$$= \tfrac{1}{2} r^2 \phi$$

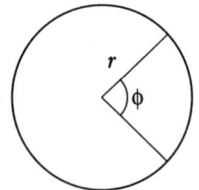

C Getting to the roots

C1 These solutions are given to two significant figures. You may have rounded yours differently.

(a) $3 \cdot 4$ (b) $2 \cdot 9$

(c) $^-2 \cdot 7$ (d) 0 and 5

For some of these the 'power' key on your calculator may be useful.

C2 The angles in these equations are all measured in radians.

(a) 0^c, $1 \cdot 3^c$, $4 \cdot 6^c$ (b) 0^c, $1 \cdot 47^c$, $3 \cdot 14^c$, $4 \cdot 81^c$

(c) 0^c, $2 \cdot 3^c$

C3 The question is asking for the positive root(s) of $0 \cdot 2v^3 - 0 \cdot 01v^2 = 1000$ (or $0 \cdot 2v^3 - 0 \cdot 01v^2 - 1000 = 0$). The solution, to 1 decimal place, is $17 \cdot 1$ miles per hour.

C4 (a) $221°C$ (b) $259°C$

Options

- The four possible graph shapes are:

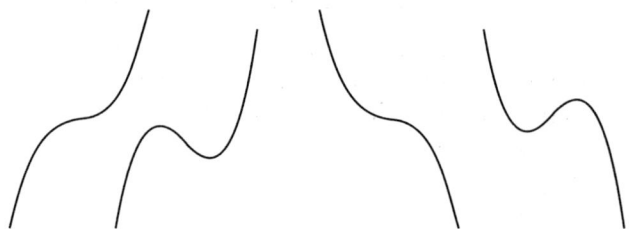

All of these shapes must cut the x-axis at least once, so a cubic always has at least one root.

- This is best shown by producing some graphs. Graphs of $y = x^n - 1$ where n is even cut the x-axis twice but only once when n is odd.

- The solution to this problem is the age at which

$$p = \frac{a(a + 5)}{100} + 107 \text{ and } p = \frac{a(3a - 10)}{500} + 120$$

intersect. The age at which this occurs is 49 years.

Mixed bag 1

1 Let the original rectangle measure a by b. It has an area of ab.

The new rectangle measures $1{\cdot}3a$ by $0{\cdot}8b$. It has an area of $1{\cdot}04ab$.

So the new rectangle's area is 4% greater than the original.

2 $138 \times 138 = 19\,044$

You can do this by using a little thought or by writing a program which tries all the possibilities. Take your pick – brains or brawn!

3 (a) $15, 0$ (b) $30, 0$
  (c) $6, 40 \left(\frac{1}{9} = \frac{400}{3600}\right)$ (d) $0, 40 \left(\frac{1}{90} = \frac{40}{3600}\right)$

4

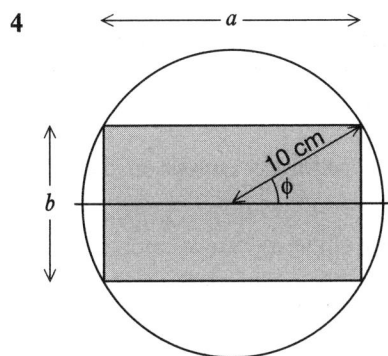

Let the rectangle measure a cm by b cm.
$$a = 2 \times 10 \cos \phi$$
and $b = 2 \times 10 \sin \phi$

So the area is $(2 \times 10 \cos \phi) \times (2 \times 10 \sin \phi)$
$$= 400 \cos \phi \sin \phi$$

The maximum area rectangle will be the one whose value of ϕ gives the maximum value of $\cos \phi \sin \phi$.

One way to do this is to plot values of $(\cos \phi \sin \phi)$ for different values of ϕ. The value of ϕ which gives a maximum is $45°$. This can only occur when the rectangle is a square.

5 $n = \dfrac{x - 42}{7}$

One of the ways to solve problems like these is by trial and adjustment – always check your final answer.

6 You need to experiment in order to find a pattern. The last digits repeat with the pattern 1, 5, 9, 5. If n is divisible by 4 the last digit of $3^n - 2^n$ is 5. If n is divided by 4 and the remainder is 1 the last digit is 1, for a remainder of 2 the last digit is 5, and for a remainder of 3 the last digit is 9. So the last digit of $3^{123} - 2^{123}$ is 9 ($123 \div 4$ has a remainder of 3).

Using remainders to look at number patterns can be very useful.

7 The volume of a pyramid or cone is
$$\frac{\text{base area} \times \text{height}}{3}.$$

Volumes of these solids can only be numerically the same as their base area when the height is 3 units.

8 The area between the x-axis and the lines $y = x$ and $x + 3y = 12$ is 18 square units.

9 Half of the square is shaded. (Divide the square up into four quarters – the curved shaded regions add up to two of these.)

10 Some of the results from Chapter 1, 'Angles and circles', will be useful here. The diagram shows one method of finding the angles in the quadrilateral. In this case, the angle at the centre is $5 \times 30° = 150°$. So the angle at the circumference is $150° \div 2 = 75°$.

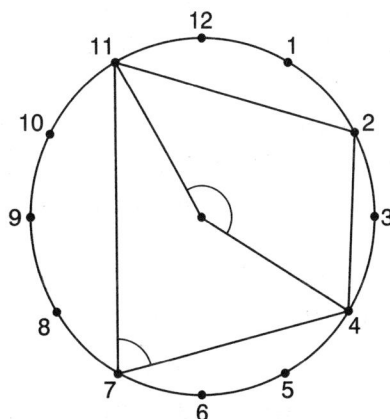

The other three internal angles of the quadrilateral are $75°$, $105°$ and $105°$.

6 Congruency

Congruency was first introduced in *Book YR*+ (Chapter 2, 'Congruent triangles'). This chapter develops the topic further. The conditions for congruency are used in simple geometrical proofs. Experience has shown that some students find this difficult; some of this chapter could be done in a small group setting. Reference is made to the conditions for congruency for other polygons. This topic could form the basis of an interesting co-operative investigation.

Section A reviews the standard conditions for congruent triangles. *Cabri-géomètre* (University of Grenoble, available from Chartwell-Bratt) or *The Geometer's Sketchpad* (Key Curriculum Press, available from Capedia) could be used to demonstrate these. Congruency is used in proving geometrical facts in Section B. Some attention is also given to the drawing of diagrams from written information rather than from prepared diagrams. This is a worthwhile skill which needs practice.

A Some recapping

A1 $\triangle$ABC is congruent to $\triangle$QRP.   (SAS)
$\triangle$DEF is congruent to $\triangle$NOM.   (ASA)

A2 No, if two quadrilaterals have their corresponding sides equal in length, they are not necessarily congruent. Imagine two quadrilaterals with their sides made from strips; although their corresponding sides are equal they can be different.

Thinking point

Two rectangles with the same area and same perimeter are congruent.
But if two triangles have the same area and perimeter it does not *necessarily* mean that they are congruent. Imagine a loop of string forming triangles with a fixed perimeter. It may be possible to make two different (non-congruent) triangles having the same area from the loop of string as shown in the diagram.

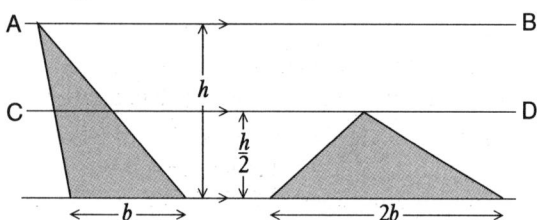

B Using congruent triangles

There may be more than one method to answer some of these questions – if in doubt ask your teacher.

B1 ABCD is a rectangle.

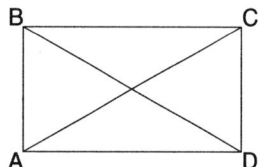

In the triangles ABD and ABC:
AB is common to both triangles.
AD = BC   (ABCD is a rectangle)
$\angle$DAB = $\angle$ABC = 90° (ABCD is a rectangle)
$\triangle$ABD and $\triangle$BAC are congruent (SAS).

So BD = AC   (corresponding sides of two congruent triangles)
$\therefore$ The diagonals of a rectangle are equal in length.

B2 ABCD is a rhombus whose diagonals cross at E.

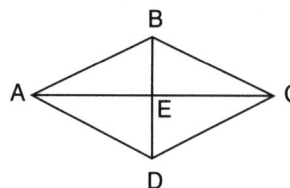

In triangles BAD and BCD:
BA = BC   (ABCD is a rhombus)
AD = CD   (ABCD is a rhombus)
BD is common to both triangles.
So triangles BAD and BCD are congruent (SSS).

In triangles ABE and CBE:
AB = BC   (ABCD is a rhombus)
BE is common to both triangles.
$\angle$ABE = $\angle$EBC   ($\triangle$ABD and $\triangle$CBD are congruent)
$\therefore$ $\triangle$ABE and $\triangle$CBE are congruent (SAS).
$\therefore$ AE = EC   (corresponding sides of congruent triangles)
$\angle$AEB = $\angle$BEC   (corresponding angles of congruent triangles)
These two angles are on a straight line, so they must both be right-angles.
This means that the diagonal BD bisects AC at right-angles.

A similar result may be proved for the diagonal AC cutting BD.
So the diagonals of a rhombus bisect each other at right-angles.

B3

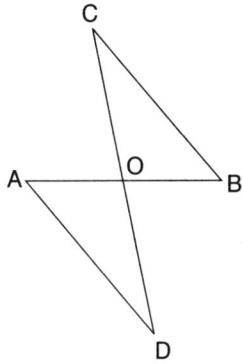

You have been given the facts that AO = OB and CO = OD.

∠AOD = ∠COB because they are opposite angles.

The triangles BOC and AOD are congruent (SAS), so CB = AD (corresponding sides of two congruent triangles).

B4

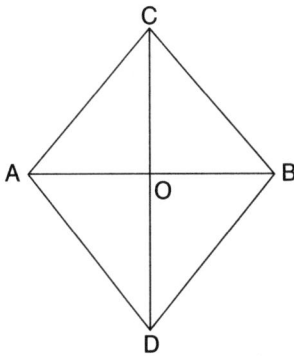

Triangles AOC and BOC are congruent (SAS), so AC = CB (corresponding sides).

Triangles COB and DOB are congruent (SAS), so BC = BD (corresponding sides).

Triangles AOD and BOD are also congruent (SAS), so AD = BD (corresponding sides).

∴ AC = CB = BD = AD

B5

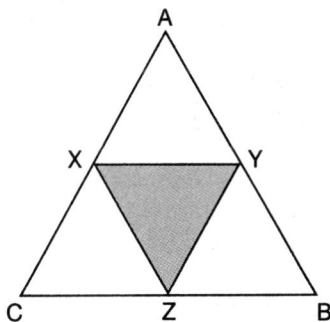

From the given conditions:
AX, XC, AY, YB, BZ, ZC are the same. Because ABC is an equilateral triangle, the angles at A, B and C are the same (60°).

The triangles CXZ, BZY and AYX are congruent to each other (SAS).

Therefore XZ = ZY = YX (corresponding sides of congruent triangles).
So XYZ must be an equilateral triangle.

B6 In ΔRQX and ΔRQY:
∠PRQ = ∠PQR (PRQ is an isosceles triangle)
RQ is common to each triangle.
QX = RY   (given)
∴ ΔRQX and ΔQRY are congruent (SAS).
∴ XR = YQ   (corresponding sides of congruent triangles)

B7 Draw a line from X to A and X to B.

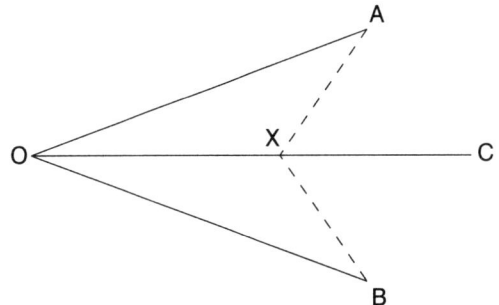

In ΔOXA and ΔOXB:
∠AOX = ∠BOX   (OC bisects ∠BOX)
OB = OA   (given)
OX is common to each triangle.
∴ ΔOXA and ΔOXB are congruent (SAS).
∴ XA = XB   (corresponding sides of congruent triangles)

B8

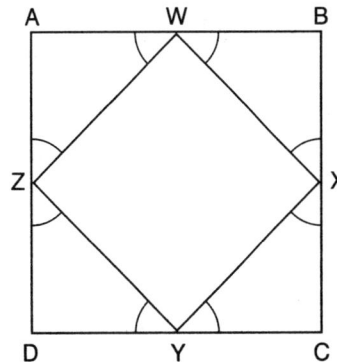

All the marked angles are 45°.
Because the sum of angles on a straight line is 180°, all the interior angles of the quadrilateral are 90°.

The triangles ZAW, WBX, XCY and YDZ are congruent (SAS). This means that the corresponding sides ZW, WX, XY and YZ are equal.
Therefore ZWXY is a square.

31

B9 There are two possible arrangements of two congruent triangles as shown.

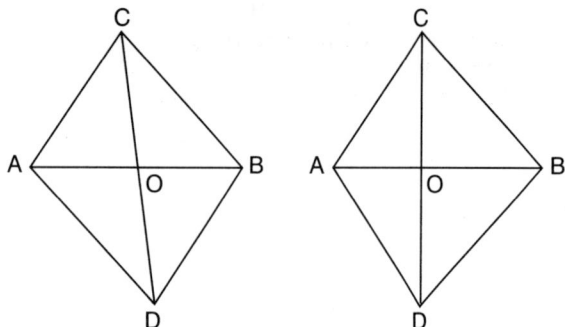

For the left-hand case:
In $\triangle$BOC and $\triangle$AOD:
  CB = AD   (corresponding sides of the congruent triangles ABC and ABD)
  $\angle$COB = $\angle$AOD   (vertically opposite angles)
  $\angle$CBO = $\angle$DAO   (corresponding angles of the congruent triangles ABC and ABD)
  $\therefore \angle$OCB = $\angle$ODA (angles in a triangle sum to 180°)
So $\triangle$BOC and $\triangle$AOD are congruent (ASA).
$\therefore$ CO = OD   (corresponding sides of the congruent triangles BOC and AOD)

For the right-hand case:
In $\triangle$BOC and $\triangle$BOD:
  CB = BD   (corresponding sides of the congruent triangles ABC and ABD)
  OB is common to both triangles.
  $\angle$CBO = $\angle$DBO   (corresponding angles of the congruent triangles ABC and ABD)
So $\triangle$BOC and $\triangle$BOD are congruent (SAS).
$\therefore$ CO = OD   (corresponding sides of the congruent triangles BOC and BOD)

B10 D is the mid-point of CB.

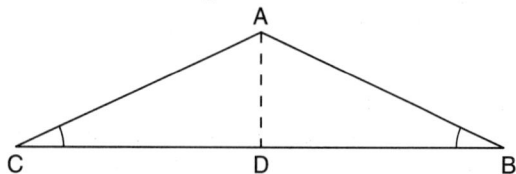

In $\triangle$ACD and $\triangle$ABD:
  AC = AB   ($\triangle$ABC is isosceles)
  $\angle$ACD = $\angle$ABD   ($\triangle$ABC is isosceles)
  CD = DB   (given)
So $\triangle$ACD and $\triangle$ABD are congruent (SAS).
$\therefore \angle$CAD = $\angle$BAD   (corresponding angles of congruent triangles)
$\angle$ADC = $\angle$ADB   (corresponding angles of congruent triangles)
But $\angle$ADC + $\angle$ADB = 180°   (angles on a straight line)
So $\angle$ADC and $\angle$ADB are both right-angles.
Therefore AD bisects $\angle$BAC and is perpendicular to BC.

B11

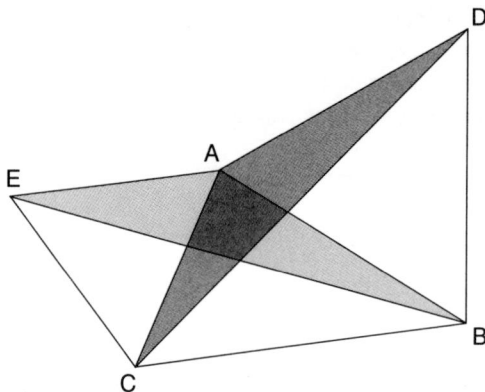

The first step with problems like this is to find the two triangles whose congruency will solve it. Two triangles which look as if they may be congruent and have BE and CD in them are EAB and CAD.
In $\triangle$EAB and $\triangle$CAD:
  EA = CA   (EAC is an equilateral triangle)
  AD = AB   (ADB is an equilateral triangle)
  $\angle$EAB = $\angle$EAC + $\angle$CAB
  but $\angle$EAC = 60°   (EAC is an equilateral triangle)
  so $\angle$EAB = 60° + $\angle$CAB
  $\angle$CAD = $\angle$DAB + $\angle$CAB
  but $\angle$DAB = 60°   (ADB is an equilateral triangle)
  so $\angle$CAD = 60° + $\angle$CAB
  $\therefore \angle$EAB = $\angle$CAD
So $\triangle$EAB and $\triangle$CAD are congruent (SAS).
$\therefore$ BE = CD   (corresponding sides of the congruent triangles EAB and CAD)

B12 In $\triangle$OXP and $\triangle$OYP:
  OY = OX   (radii of the same circle)
  XP = YP   (radii of the same circle)
  OP is common to both triangles.
So $\triangle$OXP and $\triangle$OYP are congruent (SSS).
$\therefore \angle$POX = $\angle$POY   (corresponding angles of the congruent triangles OXP and OYP)
$\therefore$ OP bisects $\angle$AOB.

B13 The lines AP, PB, BQ and QA are all equal   (radii of same or equal circles).

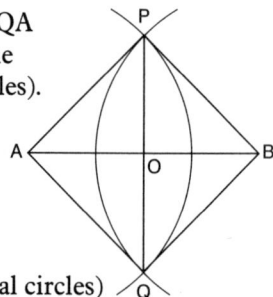

PQ is common to triangles PAQ and PBQ.
So $\triangle$PAQ and $\triangle$PBQ are congruent (SSS).

In $\triangle$PAO and $\triangle$PBO:
  PA = PB   (radii of equal circles)
  $\angle$APO = $\angle$BPO   (corresponding angles of the congruent triangles PAQ and PBQ)
  PO is common to both triangles.
So $\triangle$PAO and $\triangle$PBO are congruent (SAS).
$\therefore$ AO = OB   (corresponding sides of the congruent triangles PAO and PBO)
So the line AB is bisected by the line PQ.
(O is the mid-point of AB)

B14 The hexagon is made up of six congruent (SSS) equilateral triangles (all sides are radii of the same or equal circles). Therefore the hexagon must be regular (all sides and interior angles equal).

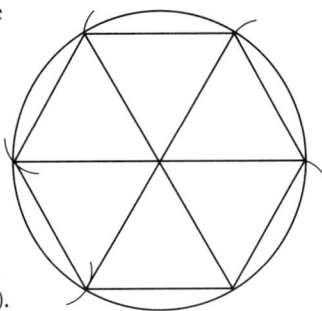

C Odds and ends

C1 Your own reasons to support these answers:
(a) The triangles are congruent (SSS).
(b) The triangles are congruent (ASA).
(c) The triangles are congruent (ASA).

C2 In $\triangle ABX$ and $\triangle CBD$:
$\angle XBA = \angle CBD$ (vertically opposite angles)
$AB = BC$ (given in the instructions)
$\angle XAB = \angle DCB = 90°$ (given in the instructions)
So $\triangle ABX$ and $\triangle CBD$ are congruent (ASA).
$\therefore CD = XA (= d)$ (corresponding sides of the congruent triangles ABX and CBD)

C3 (a) The sides of a square are all equal.
(b) Remember diagonals of rhombuses bisect each other at right-angles.

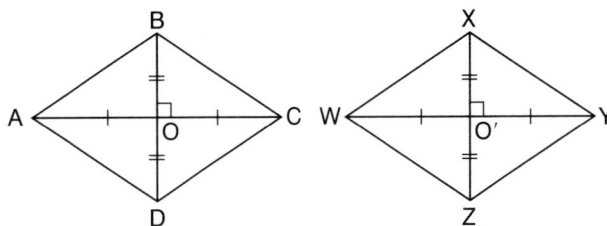

ABCD and WXYZ are the two rhombuses. Each rhombus is made from four congruent triangles (SSS, RHS or SAS). But for the same reasons these triangles are each congruent to the corresponding one in the other rhombus. Therefore the rhombuses are themselves congruent.

(c)

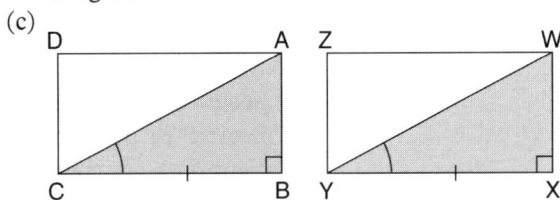

The two triangles (ABC and WXY) making half of each rectangle are congruent (ASA) and they are each congruent to the other triangle in the rectangle, so the rectangles must be congruent.

Option

There are many different ways to investigate the conditions for congruency of polygons; most of them involve splitting the polygon up into triangles and using the conditions for triangles to be congruent.

As a result, you should consider diagonal lengths, angles between diagonals, and angles between diagonals and sides.

7 Good fit?

This chapter looks at the fitting of experimental data to a linear relationship, transforming as necessary, in order to find the relationship between the two variables concerned. In many respects, it is a re-visit to the work already encountered in *Book Y5* new edition (Chapter 8, 'Equations and graphs'), although there is more emphasis on looking at and plotting the original figures in order to see what the relationship *might be*. Students should have access to a point- or graph-plotting device so that they can experiment with different relationships without the chore of manually re-plotting the points. The concept of an empirical relationship is touched upon. (There is obviously scope here for cross-curricular links with Science and Social sciences.)

In Section A the concepts of a linear relationship and line of best fit are reviewed. Students are asked to consider, at an informal level, how to quantify a line of best fit. It is not intended that this be extended into a rigorous treatment of the method of least squares. However, use of a spreadsheet to quantify the difference between expected (from the fitted relationship) and observed points is suggested. Section B concerns the proportional symbol and terms like 'constant of proportionality', 'inversely proportional to' and 'inverse square'. Some of these terms will have been met before; however, this is a useful point at which to draw them together. In Section C the idea of an empirical relationship is introduced. For this section use could be made of software or calculators which plot lines of best fit. However, care should be taken that use of such devices is not perceived as 'magic'. Some time could perhaps be devoted to discussing how and when to use such software.

A   In line

Your calculator or graphing software may have the facility to draw lines of best fit. Check your manual to find out.

A1 An approximate equation linking d and w is
$d = 2 \cdot 6w$.
Why is it only an approximate equation?

Options
Your own results and conclusions about how good people are at fitting by eye.

Thinking point
Can you think of any other methods of finding the line of best fit? Show your method to someone else to see what they think of it.

A2 (a) The sum of the deviations increases for trial gradients of $2 \cdot 5$ (sum $= 1 \cdot 25$) and $2 \cdot 7$ (sum $= {}^{-}2 \cdot 65$). So $2 \cdot 6$ is probably the best estimate of the gradient.
(b) A figure of $2 \cdot 564$ might appear to give a better fit, but it would be ridiculous to pretend that an accuracy of 1 part in $10\,000$ was possible, which is implied by this figure.

A3 (a)

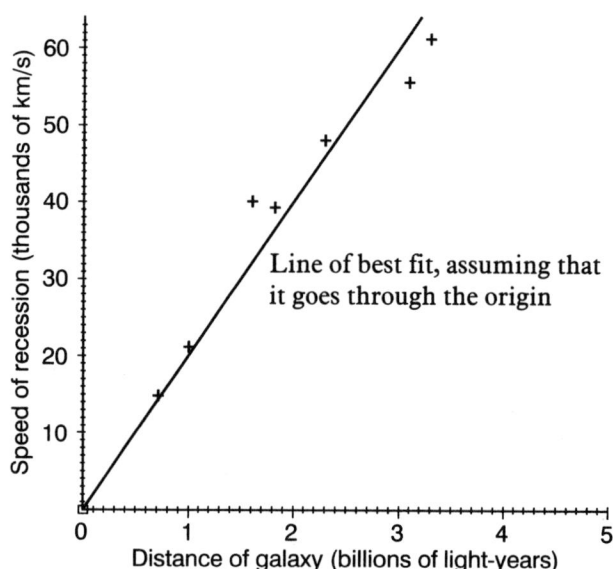

Line of best fit, assuming that it goes through the origin

(b) The gradient of the line of best fit is approximately $20\,000$ km/s per billion light-years; your figure may be slightly different to this.
(c) $v = Hx$, where $H = 20\,000$ km/s per billion light-years.
The best estimates of the Hubble constant range from about $15\,000$ to $25\,000$ km/s per billion light-years. This is because of the difficulty of measuring such vast distances accurately. The value of H is very important as it predicts whether or not the universe will go on expanding forever or eventually fall back in on itself.

(d) 1 km/s is equivalent to about 3×10^7 km/year.
1 billion light-years is equivalent to about 1×10^{22} km.
For the Hydra galaxy:
time to travel 2·8 billion light-years
$\approx \dfrac{2\cdot8 \times 1 \times 10^{22}}{60\,000 \times 3 \times 10^7}$ years $\approx 1\cdot6 \times 10^{10}$ years.

Here are some of the tabulated values for the age of the universe.

Distance (billions of light-years)	Speed of recession (thousands of km/s)	Age of universe (in units of 10^{10} years)
0·7	14·8	1·6
1·0	21·4	1·6
1·6	40·0	1·3
1·8	39·0	1·5
2·3	48·8	1·6
3·1	55·8	1·9
3·3	61·4	1·8

The mean value for the age of the universe is about $1\cdot6 \times 10^{10}$ years.

According to a book on astronomy:
'Taking the Hubble constant as 15 000 km/s per billion light-years, the time since the galaxies began to move apart would be a billion light-years divided by 15 000 km/s or 20 thousand million years.' Why is this true?

B Using the $\propto$ symbol

B1 (a) y is proportional to x; $y = 0\cdot4x$.
(b) y is not proportional to x.
(c) y is not proportional to x.
(d) y is proportional to x; $y = 0\cdot25x$.

B2 Some of your own examples of quantities that are either directly or inversely proportional to each other. Two examples are: cost of petrol is directly proportional to amount bought; journey time is inversely proportional to average speed.

B3 (a) $y \propto x^2$, $y = kx^2$ or $y = 2x^2$
(b) $y \propto x$, $y = kx$ or $y = 2x$
(c) $y \propto \dfrac{1}{x}$, $y = \dfrac{k}{x}$ or $y = \dfrac{12}{x}$
(d) no obvious connection
(e) $y \propto x^2$, $y = kx^2$ or $y = x^2$
(f) $y \propto \dfrac{1}{x^2}$, $y = \dfrac{k}{x^2}$ or $y = \dfrac{72}{x^2}$

B4 (a) $t \propto d$ t represents increase in temperature, d the depth underground.
(b) $v \propto r^3$ v represents volume of the sphere, r the radius of the sphere.
(c) $f \propto \dfrac{1}{d^2}$ f represents the force, d the distance apart of the masses.
(You may have used different letters.)

C Fit for what?

Thinking point
The number of VCRs owned depends also on the standard of living; no matter how cheap they are, if people do not have the money they cannot buy them. It might also depend on new films being released on tape or the time of year; for example, people might want to record a special event like the Olympics.

Thinking point
The data is only available down to a cost of £150. Below this cost you cannot assume that the empirical rule still holds. At a cost below £85, the empirical rule gives a percentage over 100%, which is clearly wrong.

C1 (a) A plot of q against p^2 should give a straight line of gradient a.
(b) A plot of q^2 against p^3 should give a straight line of gradient a.
(c) A plot of q against $\dfrac{1}{p^2}$ should give a straight line of gradient a and intercept b.
(d) A plot of $\dfrac{1}{q}$ against p^2 should give a straight line of gradient a and intercept b.

C2 Your figures may be slightly different to the ones here.
The gradient of the line of best fit is 9·6, but as the x-axis has been enlarged by a factor of 100 the 'true' gradient is 960. (*Make sure that you understand why.*)

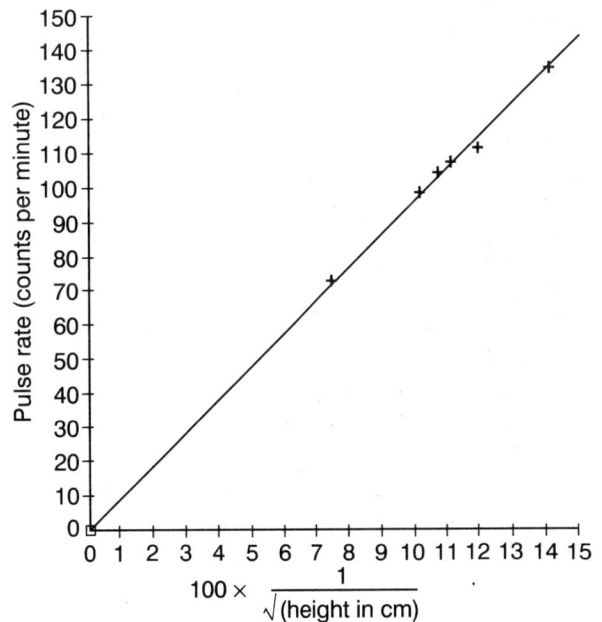

(Note the change in the x-axis scale; all values are × 100.)

According to the fitted straight line the relationship between pulse rate (y) in beats per minute and height (x) in cm is $y = \dfrac{960}{\sqrt{x}}$.

It is sometimes useful to compare the experimental or observed figures with those predicted by the fitted relationship. Here is the spreadsheet output for these observations and the fitted results; it also gives the percentage difference between observed and fitted pulse rates. The fitted empirical relationship fits the observed pulse rates very well.

Height (cm)	Observed pulse	Fitted pulse (1 d.p.)	% difference (1 d.p.)
50	134	135.8	−1.3
69.8	111	114.9	−3.5
79.6	108	107.6	0.4
86.7	104	103.1	0.9
98.6	98	96.7	1.3
176.5	73	72.3	1.0

C3 When you are not quite sure what the relationship might be it is usually a good idea to plot the points as they stand. For the case here one of the points must be the origin – obviously when the earthmover is stationary there can be no temperature rise.

You could use a graph-plotter to do your initial 'sketch'. This should suggest that it is worth plotting rise over air temperature ($t\,°C$) against $\sqrt{\text{(speed of earthmover (s km/h))}}$ to fit the empirical relationship $t = a\sqrt{s}$, where a is a constant.

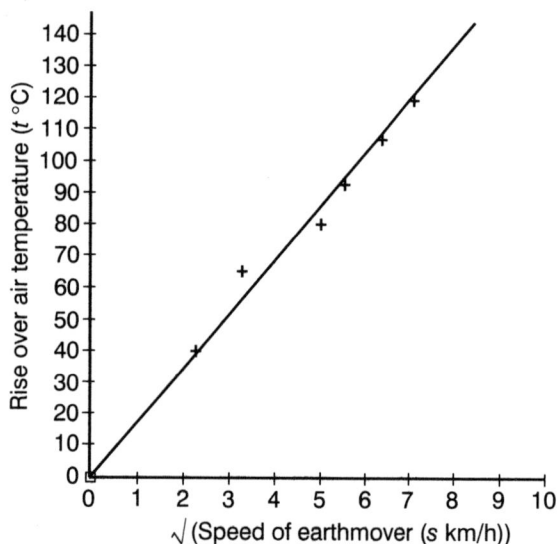

The gradient of the fitted line $\approx 17{\cdot}4$ so the empirical relationship is $t \approx 17{\cdot}4\,\sqrt{s}$. Assuming that the empirical relationship is valid for a speed of 60 km/h (this is outside the range of the experimental figures so we need to be cautious), the temperature rise to the nearest °C should be 135 °C.

C4 If Kepler's third law is true, plotting (moon orbit radius)^3 against (time for one orbit)^2 should give a straight line. The problem with the results here is that they split into two distinct groups: one for Ganymede and Callisto, and one for Leda, Himalia and Lysitha. With a graph-plotter it is possible to look easily at both sets of figures by altering the scale but keeping the same gradient for the fitted line. This is shown below and in fact the fit is excellent. But for situations where you have control of the values the variables may take (which is impossible in astronomy!), it is always a good idea to try to have evenly-spaced values after they have been transformed.

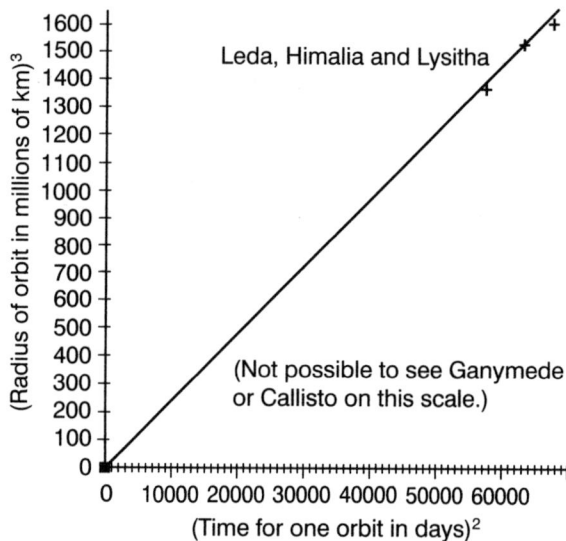

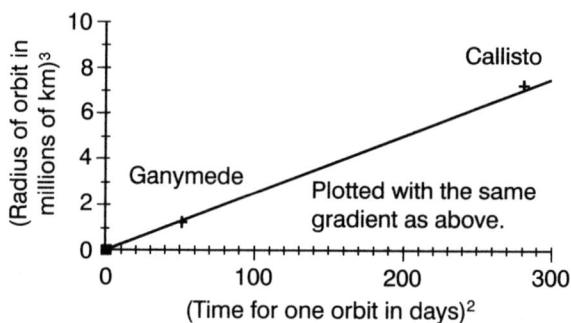

C5 Plotting deceleration against impact speed should give a curve which suggests a quadratic relationship, $y \propto x^2$.

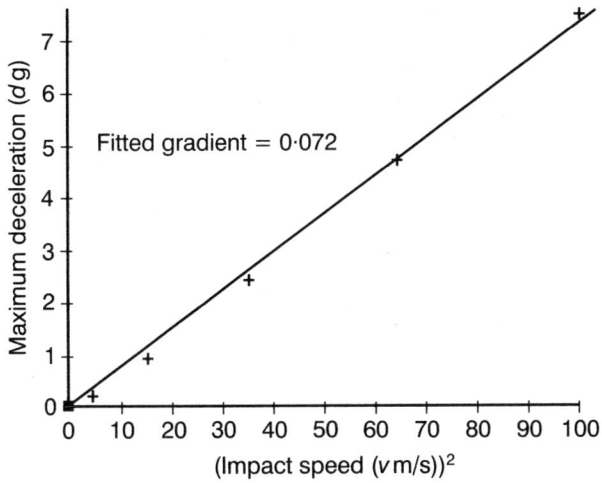

An empirical formula connecting the impact speed (v m/s) of the model with its deceleration (d m/s^2) is $d = 0.072v^2$.

C6 Plotting expenditure against income should give a curve which suggests a relationship of the form $y \propto \sqrt{x}$. The empirical relationship is of the form $y = a\sqrt{x}$. The gradient = 1.7, so $y = 1.7\sqrt{x}$.

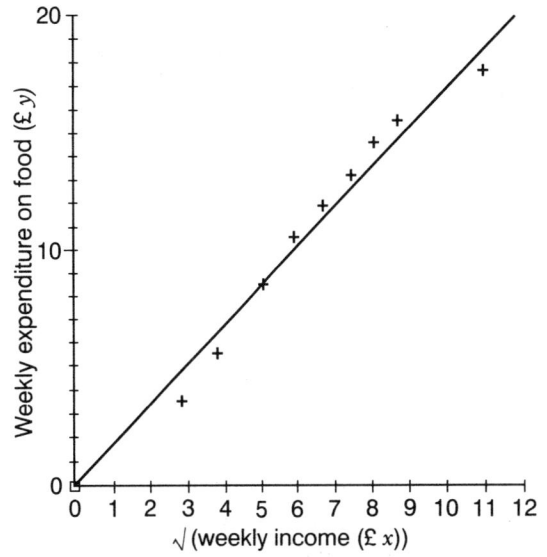

Option

Carol is right.

Your own checks on some of the graphs in this chapter

Mixed bag 2

1 The sides of the cuboid measure, in cm, 4, 6 and 8. Therefore the cuboid has a volume of 192 cm³.
Why not make up and try some similar problems yourself?

2 The number is 6. (An alternative answer is 1, although this is harder to find.)
There are several other numbers such that the result of adding a second number to them gives a result whose square root is the original number less the second number. Here are some of them (the difference is given after the number itself):
6 (10), 15 (10), 15 (21), 21 (28).

3 When a negative (or positive) number is squared the result is a positive number, so the square root of a positive number can be either positive or negative. This does not mean that the positive root is equal to the negative root.

4 The prefix 'micro' means millionth.
In a century there are (ignoring leap years)
$100 \times 365 \times 24 = 876\,000$ hours which is
0.876×10^6, so a micro-century is
0.876 hours ≈ 50 minutes.

5 (a) In this section of spreadsheet, the approximate value of $\sqrt{2}$ becomes the next estimate (a).

x	a	Approximate x^0.5	Accurate value	% difference
2	1.5	1.4375	1.41421356237309505	−1.646599
2	1.4375	1.42036290322580645	1.41421356237309505	−0.434824
2	1.4203629032	1.4158244962323258	1.41421356237309505	−0.113910
2	1.4158244962	1.41463466800419611	1.41421356237309505	−0.029776
2	1.4146346680	1.41432357891256698	1.41421356237309505	−0.007779
2	1.4143235789	1.41424230062934465	1.41421356237309505	−0.002032
2	1.4142423006	1.41422106902001418	1.41421356237309505	−5.308E-4
2	1.41422010000	1.41421550014500705	1.41421056007000505	1.000E-4
2	1.4142155231	1.41421407453489546	1.41421356237309505	−3.621E-5

Only a few iterations are needed before a very accurate value of $\sqrt{2}$ is arrived at.
What happens if the first estimate is 1? Can all square roots be found starting with 1?
This method of finding approximate square roots was being used by Arab mathematicians in the 13th century.

(b) The approximation $\tan x = \dfrac{10 + x}{100 - x}$ is valid when x is measured in degrees in the range between 25° to 65°. You could use a spreadsheet similar to the one shown in part (a).

(c) $\sin x \approx x$ is a good approximation for small values of x, which must be in radians. For $x < 0.25$, the difference between approximate and accurate value is less than 1%.

6 (a) The letter 'H'   (b) The letter 'M'

7 The statement is true. This spreadsheet shows the situation for the set of numbers (1, 2, 2, 11, 19, 25), median 6·5.

Numbers	Absolute deviation from	
	6.5	
1	5.5	
2	4.5	
2	4.5	
11	4.5	
19	12.5	
25	18.5	
	50	= Sum of absolute deviations

Remember that showing that something is true for a few cases does not prove it.

Experiment with different numbers from which the sum of the absolute deviations are calculated. You could write a program which does the same job.

8 Making possibility space diagrams of A against B, B against C and so on will show that Roy is correct. For example, here is the probability space diagram for A against B. The letters give the winner.

Score on dice B

		3	3	3	3	3	3
	4	A	A	A	A	A	A
	4	A	A	A	A	A	A
Score	4	A	A	A	A	A	A
on	4	A	A	A	A	A	A
dice A	0	B	B	B	B	B	B
	0	B	B	B	B	B	B

A will beat B $\frac{2}{3}$ of the time.

9 The dealer is not telling the truth. In fact the probability of the dealer winning is greater than the 0·5 it seems at first. To see why, label each side of a card 1 or 2. Card A is white on one side, black on the other; card B is black on both sides; card C is white on both sides.

The common mistake is to forget that although card B is black on both sides there are two different ways it can be placed. They both give black top and bottom face, but there are two different ways of this occurring (imagine each face was labelled). The card the dealer takes shows black so it cannot be the white–white card C. The table below shows all the possibilities; the shaded ones no longer apply.

	Card A		Card B		Card C	
Top face	White (1)	Black (2)	Black (1)	Black (2)	White (1)	White (2)
Bottom face	Black (2)	White (1)	Black (2)	Black (1)	White (2)	White (1)

Looking at the table there are three possibilities; of these, two give the bottom face as black. So the bottom face is more likely to be black – it is not a fair game.

10 (a) Providing the coin is fair, heads and tails have equal probabilities, so it does not matter who does the calling.

(b) Precisely where a cannon ball lands is independent of where the previous one landed, so the sailor is equally likely to be hit wherever he is on the ship.

11 One way to test the hypothesis that tomorrow's weather is likely to be like today's would be to collect weather records from a daily newspaper going back over at least several weeks. (You may need to reduce this data to perhaps four or five types of weather, such as sunny, showery, snow and so on.) From this information make a tally of the times when two consecutive days had the same weather or when the weather was different and compare these frequencies.

8 Angles and circles 2

This chapter continues with the elementary geometrical properties met with in Chapter 1 ('Angles and circles 1'). The properties considered here are those relating to tangents to circles. As before, there is scope for students to use *Cabri-géomètre* (University of Grenoble, available from Chartwell-Bratt) or *The Geometer's Sketchpad* (Key Curriculum Press, available from Capedia).

Section A begins with a short review of some of the technical terms associated with the circle including arc, chord, inscribed, sector, segment, subtend and tangent. There are questions involving drawing and measurement relating to circles and tangents and some loci work. These should give students a 'feel' as to what a tangent is. (They may have already encountered tangents to curves in Chapter 3 ('Tangents to curves').)

In Section B some more formal aspects of tangents to circles are considered. These include 'tangents from the same point to a circle are equal, subtend equal angles at the circle centre and make equal angles with the straight line joining the point to the circle.' The equality of the angle between a tangent and a chord with the angle in the alternate segment is also encountered. Students then have to find various angles and give reasons for each step in their working. They are also asked to prove some simple properties relating to circles, tangents and curves.

A   Technical terms – a review

A1 Any chord which is a diameter of a circle is a line of symmetry.

A2 (a) The centres of the circles lie on the perpendicular bisector of the line joining the two points.

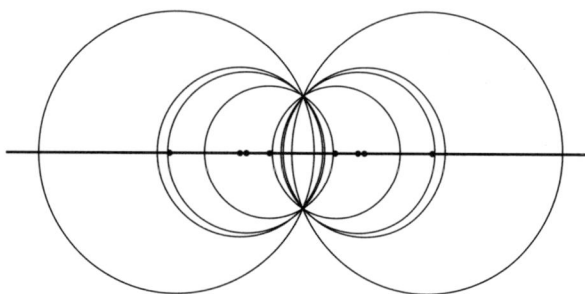

(b) (i)

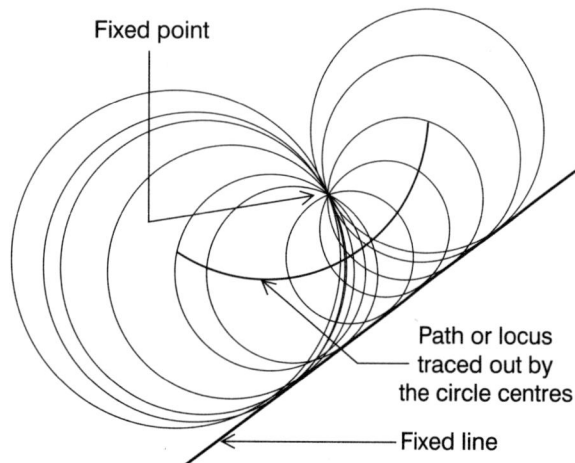

Fixed point

Path or locus traced out by the circle centres

Fixed line

(ii) The centres of circles which touch two straight lines lie on the bisector of the angle between the two lines.

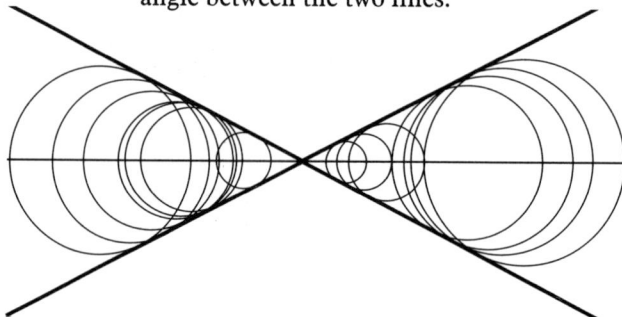

(iii) There is only one circle which can pass through three points!

A3 Looking at the symmetry of the situation and using the result from **A2**, the centre of the circle must lie on the lines bisecting *each* angle.

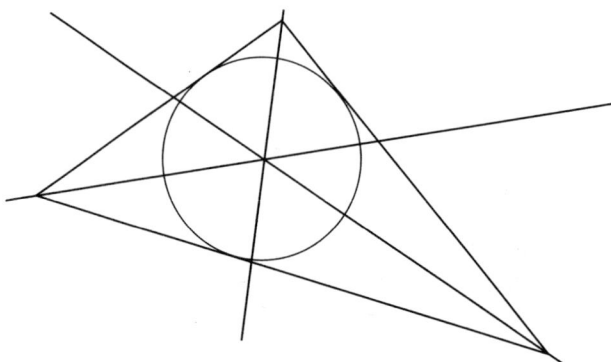

A4 Join the endpoints of the arc with a straight line. Find the perpendicular bisector of this line. This passes through the midpoint of the arc (and the centre of the circle).

A5 You should have found that, within experimental error, AX × XB = CX × XD.

A6 You should have found (again, within experimental error) that the radius of the circle is half the difference between the hypotenuse and the other two sides, or:
$$r = \tfrac{1}{2}(a + b - h)$$

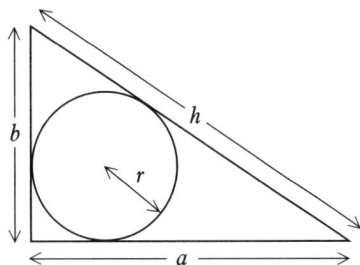

A7 The pairs of lines AA′, CC′ and BB′, DD′ are parallel.

Before starting the proof it is useful to prove another fact about cyclic quadrilaterals.

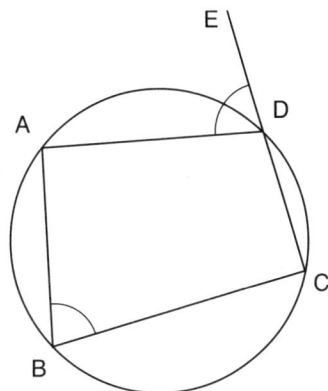

ABCD is a cyclic quadrilateral,
so ∠ABC + ∠ADC = 180° (opposite angles of a cyclic quadrilateral)
but ∠ADE + ∠ADC = 180° (angles on a straight line sum to 180°)
∴ ∠ABC = ∠ADE
This result is sometimes stated as 'the external angle of a cyclic quadrilateral is equal to the interior opposite angle.'
This means that the angles marked with the same letter are equal in size.

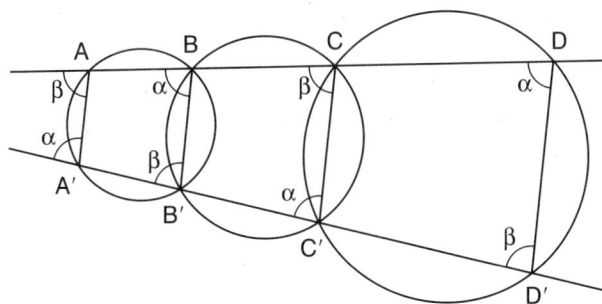

ABB′A′, BCC′B′ and CDD′C′ are all cyclic quadrilaterals.
∠ABB′ = ∠CDD′ = α
∴ BB′ is parallel to DD′. (*Why?*)
Similarly, ∠BAA′ = ∠DCC′ = β
∴ AA′ is parallel to CC′. (*Why?*)

B Tangents to a circle

B1 (a) $a = 90° - 30°$ (angle in isosceles triangle and
    $= 60°$ angle between radius and tangent)

(b) $b = 360° - (120° + 90° + 90°)$ (angle sum of
    $= 60°$ a quadrilateral is 360°)

(c)

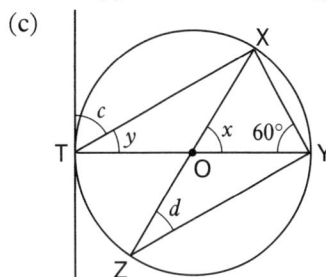

∠TOX = 2 × ∠TYX (angle at centre is
    $= 120°$ twice angle at circumference)
so $x = 180° - 120°$ (sum of angles on a line)
    $= 60°$
∴ $y = 30°$ (angle at circumference is half angle at centre)
so $d = 30°$ (angles in the same segment)
    $c = 90° - 30°$ (angle between radius and
    $= 60°$ tangent is 90°)

B2 In triangles OAT and OBT:
    ∠OAT = ∠OBT (angle between radius and
        $= 90°$ tangent)
    OA = OB (radii of a circle)
    OT is common to both triangles.
∴ ΔOAT is congruent to ΔOBT (RHS).
∴ AT = BT and (corresponding sides and
∠BTO = ∠ATO   angles of congruent triangles)

B3

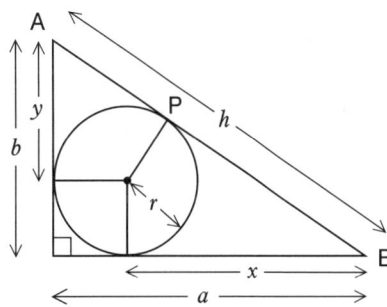

    $y = b - r$
∴ AP = $b - r$ (tangents from same point are equal in length)
    $x = a - r$
∴ BP = $a - r$ (tangents from same point are equal in length)
$h = AP + BP$
    $= (b - r) + (a - r)$
    $= a + b - 2r$
∴ $2r = a + b - h$
∴ $r = \tfrac{1}{2}((a + b) - h)$

B4

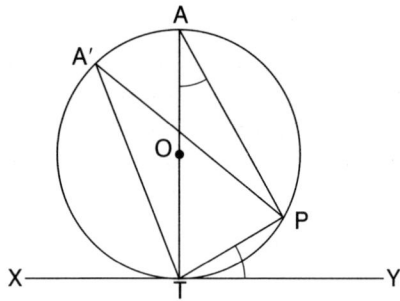

$\angle ATP = 90° - \angle PTY$ (angle between radius and tangent is 90°)

$\angle APT = 90°$ (angle in a semi-circle)

$\angle TAP = 180° - 90° - (90° - \angle PTY)$ (angles in a triangle)

$\therefore \angle TAP = \angle PTY$

Draw a new position of A – say A′.

Join A′ to P and T.

$\angle TA'P = \angle TAP$ (angles in the same segment)

$\therefore \angle TA'P = \angle PTY$

Thinking point

z is the angle in the 'other' segment.

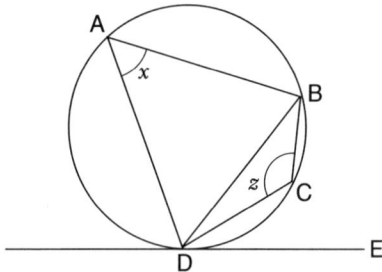

$\angle BDE = \angle DAB$

$\quad = x$ (angle between chord and tangent is equal to the angle subtended by the chord in the alternate segment, *or simply angle between chord and tangent*)

ABCD is a cyclic quadrilateral.

So $\angle DAB + \angle BCD = 180°$

$\therefore z = 180° - x$

B5 (a) $a = 60°$ (angle between chord and tangent)

$\quad b = 75°$ (angle between chord and tangent)

(b) $c = f = 60°$ (equilateral triangle)

$\quad d = 60°$ (angle between chord and tangent)

$\quad e = 180° - d - f$ (angles on a straight line)

$\quad\quad = 60°$

B6

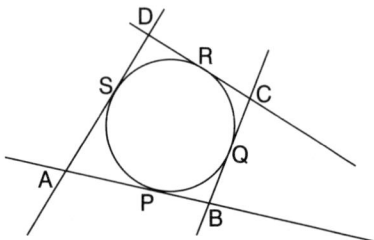

(a) AP = AS, BP = BQ, CQ = CR, DR = DS   (tangents to a circle)

$AB + CD = AP + PB + CR + RD$

$\quad\quad\quad\quad = BQ + QC + AS + SD$

$\quad\quad\quad\quad = BC + AD$

(b)

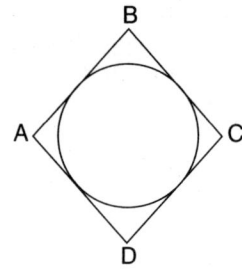

ABCD is a parallelogram, so AB = DC and AD = BC.

But in (a) it has been proved that

AB + CD = BC + AD, so all four sides must be equal in length.

B7 $\angle CBP = \angle CAB$ (angle between chord and tangent)

$\angle PCB = \angle CAB + \angle ABC$ (exterior angle of a triangle is equal to the sum of the two opposite interior angles)

$\angle ABP = \angle CBP + \angle ABC$

$\quad\quad\quad = \angle CAB + \angle ABC$

$\therefore \angle PCB = \angle ABP$

B8 (a) $\angle XYZ = 180° - (60° + 70°)$ (angles on a straight line)

$\quad\quad\quad = 50°$

$\angle XWZ = 130°$ (opposite angles in a cyclic quadrilateral sum to 180°)

$\triangle WXZ$ is isosceles.   (WZ = WX given)

So $a = b = 25°$ (angle of isosceles triangle)

(b) $\angle DBC = c$ (angle in alternate segment)

$\angle ADE = c$ (vertically opposite angles)

AB = AD   (tangents from the same point)

$\therefore \triangle ABD$ is isosceles.

Similarly, $\triangle CBD$ is isosceles.

$\angle ABD = \angle ADE = c$ (angle in alternate segment)

$\angle ADB = \angle ABD = c$ (equal angles of isosceles $\triangle ABD$)

$\angle BDC = \angle DBC = c$ (equal angles of isosceles $\triangle CBD$)

$\therefore \angle ADB + \angle BDC + c = 180°$ (angle sum on a straight line)

$\therefore c + c + c = 180°$

So $c = 60°$

B9 (There are many different ways to prove that ABCD is a rhombus.)

$\angle ADE = \angle ABD$ (angle in alternate segment)

but $\angle ADE = \angle CDF$ (vertically opposite angles)

$\angle CDF = \angle DBC$ (angle in alternate segment)

$\therefore \angle ADE = \angle DBC$

$\triangle BCD$ and $\triangle ABD$ are isosceles   (tangents from a point, AB = AD and CB = CD)

So these angles are all equal to one another:

$\angle ABD, \angle ADB, \angle DBC, \angle BDC, \angle ADE$ and $\angle CDF$

AD is parallel to BC.   *(Why?)*

AB is parallel to DC.   *(Why?)*

AB = AD, CB = CD

$\therefore$ ABCD is a rhombus.

9 Introduction to matrices

This chapter gives an introduction to matrices, including matrix addition, subtraction and multiplication. The material is not particularly challenging and could probably be attempted a year or so before the content in the rest of this book. More matrix work, including transformation matrices, is met in *Book YX2*. Further matrix work may also be found in SMP 16–19 *Matrices*.

Once students are confident with matrix addition, subtraction and multiplication it may be appropriate for them to use a suitable calculator, for example the TI–81 or TI–82, or piece of software, for example, *Matpack: exploring matrices* (Keele Mathematical Educational Publications, Keele, 1990), which includes work on 3-D and 2-D matrix geometry.

Section A introduces matrices as stores of information. This could be more relevant to students if local or school events or something similar were used. Examples which might be useful include attendance records, charity collections or amounts spent on various commodities. Matrix multiplication is introduced in Section B using the nutritional composition of various meal combinations; students could be asked to produce a well-balanced diet. A matrix-handling calculator or piece of software would encourage trial and improvement in this task. Almost all packaged foodstuffs carry nutritional information – a well-balanced sandwich would make an interesting investigation. There is scope here for cross-curricular work. The chapter concludes with an option which employs a spreadsheet to perform matrix multiplications. This is not intended as a pure spreadsheet exercise but rather to consider in detail the algebraic manipulations involved in matrix multiplications. A 'super challenge' might be to write a BASIC program to perform matrix multiplications. (Some BASIC dialects are already 'wired' with matrix arithmetic.)

A Starting matrices

A1 (a) The Glasgow factory made the most hatchbacks.
   (b) The London factory made 800 estate cars.
   (c) The total number of cars made in Glasgow was 5883.

A2 Only saloons were made in London and only hatchbacks in Glasgow. There were no estates made at all. Some production lines may have closed for the summer, perhaps there was a special order or there was a lack of some parts or …

A3 (a) The matrix showing combined sales for Monday and Tuesday is:

	R	Cass	CD
Pop	15	50	146
Jazz	8	39	18
EL	1	68	51
Class	5	8	58

   (b) The difference in sales between Tuesday and Monday.
   (c) This matrix shows the sales for Saturday.
$$\begin{bmatrix} 14 & 48 & 152 \\ 6 & 42 & 36 \\ 0 & 68 & 42 \\ 4 & 16 & 76 \end{bmatrix}$$

A4 $\underset{\sim}{T} - \underset{\sim}{M}$ represents the difference in sales between Tuesday and Monday. (*What about* $\underset{\sim}{M} - \underset{\sim}{T}$?)

A5 (a) $\underset{\sim}{M} + \underset{\sim}{M} = \begin{bmatrix} 14 & 48 & 152 \\ 6 & 42 & 36 \\ 0 & 68 & 42 \\ 4 & 16 & 76 \end{bmatrix}$

   (b) This is the same answer as (a) because $\underset{\sim}{M} + \underset{\sim}{M} = 2\underset{\sim}{M}$.

A6 $\frac{1}{2}(\underset{\sim}{M} + \underset{\sim}{T})$ represents the average (mean) sales for Monday and Tuesday, which is
$$\begin{bmatrix} 7{\cdot}5 & 25 & 73 \\ 4 & 19{\cdot}5 & 9 \\ 0{\cdot}5 & 34 & 20{\cdot}5 \\ 2{\cdot}5 & 4 & 29 \end{bmatrix}.$$

Option

See if your own calculator or software can handle calculations involving matrices. There are quite a few different ways of entering and performing matrix calculations, so it is best to check with your own manual.

A7 $\underset{\sim}{A} + \underset{\sim}{B} = \begin{bmatrix} 1 & 0 & 2 \\ 4 & 2 & 6 \end{bmatrix} + \begin{bmatrix} 2 & 4 & 0 \\ 4 & 0 & 4 \end{bmatrix}$

$= \begin{bmatrix} 3 & 4 & 2 \\ 8 & 2 & 10 \end{bmatrix}$

$\underset{\sim}{A} - \underset{\sim}{B} = \begin{bmatrix} 1 & 0 & 2 \\ 4 & 2 & 6 \end{bmatrix} - \begin{bmatrix} 2 & 4 & 0 \\ 4 & 0 & 4 \end{bmatrix}$

$= \begin{bmatrix} ^-1 & ^-4 & 2 \\ 0 & 2 & 2 \end{bmatrix}$

A8 (a) $2\underset{\sim}{A} = 2\begin{bmatrix} 1 & 0 & 2 \\ 4 & 2 & 6 \end{bmatrix} = \begin{bmatrix} 2 & 0 & 4 \\ 8 & 4 & 12 \end{bmatrix}$

(b) $2\underset{\sim}{A} + \underset{\sim}{B} = \begin{bmatrix} 2 & 0 & 4 \\ 8 & 4 & 12 \end{bmatrix} + \begin{bmatrix} 2 & 4 & 0 \\ 4 & 0 & 4 \end{bmatrix}$

$= \begin{bmatrix} 4 & 4 & 4 \\ 12 & 4 & 16 \end{bmatrix}$

(c) $\underset{\sim}{B} - \underset{\sim}{A} = \begin{bmatrix} 2 & 4 & 0 \\ 4 & 0 & 4 \end{bmatrix} - \begin{bmatrix} 1 & 0 & 2 \\ 4 & 2 & 6 \end{bmatrix}$

$= \begin{bmatrix} 1 & 4 & ^-2 \\ 0 & ^-2 & ^-2 \end{bmatrix}$

A9 Your own matrix calculations
You may be able to check them with a calculator which can perform matrix calculations or perhaps a piece of software.

B Matrix multiplication

B1 (a)
(i) $1 \times 6{\cdot}0 + 3 \times 1{\cdot}6 + 3 \times 0{\cdot}1 + 2 \times 6{\cdot}0 = 23{\cdot}1\,g$
(ii) $0 \times 6{\cdot}0 + 4 \times 1{\cdot}6 + 2 \times 0{\cdot}1 + 3 \times 6{\cdot}0 = 24{\cdot}6\,g$
(iii) $1 \times 1{\cdot}0 + 3 \times 0{\cdot}4 + 3 \times 5{\cdot}0 + 2 \times 7{\cdot}0 = 31{\cdot}2\,g$
(iv) $0 \times 1{\cdot}0 + 4 \times 0{\cdot}4 + 2 \times 5{\cdot}0 + 3 \times 7{\cdot}0 = 32{\cdot}6\,g$
Can you see the pattern in the calculations?

(b) The extra calculations needed are the amounts of carbohydrate in menus A and B:
A $1 \times 20{\cdot}0 + 3 \times 13{\cdot}7 + 3 \times 0 + 2 \times 0{\cdot}5 = 62{\cdot}1\,g$
B $0 \times 20{\cdot}0 + 4 \times 13{\cdot}7 + 2 \times 0 + 3 \times 0{\cdot}5 = 56{\cdot}3\,g$

The information can then be stored in this Menu/Nutrition matrix.

	Protein (g)	Fat (g)	Carbohydrate (g)
Menu A	23·1	31·2	62·1
Menu B	24·6	32·6	56·3

B2 (a) The amount of carbohydrate in menu B
(b) The amount of fat in menu A

B3

Addition	Allowed	Possible multiplication (orders involved)	Allowed (result)
$\underset{\sim}{A} + \underset{\sim}{B}$	No	$\underset{\sim}{A}\,\underset{\sim}{B}$ $(2 \times 3)(2 \times 2)$	No
$\underset{\sim}{A} + \underset{\sim}{C}$	No	$\underset{\sim}{A}\,\underset{\sim}{C}$ $(2 \times 3)(3 \times 2)$	Yes (2×2)
$\underset{\sim}{A} + \underset{\sim}{D}$	Yes	$\underset{\sim}{A}\,\underset{\sim}{D}$ $(2 \times 3)(2 \times 3)$	No
$\underset{\sim}{B} + \underset{\sim}{C}$	No	$\underset{\sim}{B}\,\underset{\sim}{C}$ $(2 \times 2)(3 \times 2)$	No
$\underset{\sim}{B} + \underset{\sim}{D}$	No	$\underset{\sim}{B}\,\underset{\sim}{D}$ $(2 \times 2)(2 \times 3)$	Yes (2×3)
$\underset{\sim}{C} + \underset{\sim}{D}$	No	$\underset{\sim}{C}\,\underset{\sim}{D}$ $(3 \times 2)(2 \times 3)$	Yes (3×3)
$\underset{\sim}{D} + \underset{\sim}{C}$	No	$\underset{\sim}{D}\,\underset{\sim}{C}$ $(2 \times 3)(3 \times 2)$	Yes (2×2)
$\underset{\sim}{D} + \underset{\sim}{B}$	No	$\underset{\sim}{D}\,\underset{\sim}{B}$ $(2 \times 3)(2 \times 2)$	No
$\underset{\sim}{D} + \underset{\sim}{A}$	Yes	$\underset{\sim}{D}\,\underset{\sim}{A}$ $(2 \times 3)(2 \times 3)$	No
$\underset{\sim}{C} + \underset{\sim}{B}$	No	$\underset{\sim}{C}\,\underset{\sim}{B}$ $(3 \times 2)(2 \times 2)$	Yes (3×2)
$\underset{\sim}{C} + \underset{\sim}{A}$	No	$\underset{\sim}{C}\,\underset{\sim}{A}$ $(3 \times 2)(2 \times 3)$	Yes (3×3)
$\underset{\sim}{B} + \underset{\sim}{A}$	No	$\underset{\sim}{B}\,\underset{\sim}{A}$ $(2 \times 2)(2 \times 3)$	Yes (2×3)

B4 (a) $\begin{bmatrix} 1 & 0 \\ 0 & 1 \end{bmatrix}\begin{bmatrix} 1 & 2 & 1 \\ 3 & 4 & 1 \end{bmatrix} = \begin{bmatrix} \mathbf{1} & \mathbf{2} & \mathbf{1} \\ \mathbf{3} & \mathbf{4} & \mathbf{1} \end{bmatrix}$

(b) $\begin{bmatrix} 1 & 2 \\ 2 & 1 \end{bmatrix}\begin{bmatrix} 1 & 2 \\ 2 & 1 \end{bmatrix} = \begin{bmatrix} \mathbf{5} & \mathbf{4} \\ \mathbf{4} & \mathbf{5} \end{bmatrix}$

(c) $\begin{bmatrix} 1 & 1 \\ 2 & 1 \end{bmatrix}\begin{bmatrix} 2 & 1 & 3 \\ 3 & 1 & 2 \end{bmatrix} = \begin{bmatrix} \mathbf{5} & \mathbf{2} & \mathbf{5} \\ \mathbf{7} & \mathbf{3} & \mathbf{8} \end{bmatrix}$

(d) $\begin{bmatrix} 1 & 0 & 0 \\ 1 & 0 & 1 \\ 1 & 1 & 1 \end{bmatrix}\begin{bmatrix} 1 & 2 \\ 2 & 1 \\ 1 & 1 \end{bmatrix} = \begin{bmatrix} \mathbf{1} & \mathbf{2} \\ \mathbf{2} & \mathbf{3} \\ \mathbf{4} & \mathbf{4} \end{bmatrix}$

B5 Providing the multiplication is possible, multiplying by $\begin{bmatrix} 1 & 0 \\ 0 & 1 \end{bmatrix}$ does not change the matrix it multiplies.

B6 Multiplying by $\begin{bmatrix} 2 & 0 \\ 0 & 2 \end{bmatrix}$ doubles each element in the second matrix, if the multiplication is possible.

B7 Squaring a 2×3 means multiplying a 2×3 by a 2×3. But the rules for matrix multiplication state that the number of columns of the first matrix must equal the number of rows of the second matrix. Therefore it is not possible to square a 2×3 matrix.

B8 No, it is not correct because in matrix multiplication elements of the first row in the first matrix are multiplied by elements of the first column in the second matrix and so on.

$\begin{bmatrix} 2 & 4 \\ 1 & 3 \end{bmatrix}\begin{bmatrix} 2 & 4 \\ 1 & 3 \end{bmatrix} = \begin{bmatrix} 2 \times 2 + 4 \times 1 & 2 \times 4 + 4 \times 3 \\ 1 \times 2 + 3 \times 1 & 1 \times 4 + 3 \times 3 \end{bmatrix}$

$= \begin{bmatrix} 8 & 20 \\ 5 & 13 \end{bmatrix}$

B9 Here are some examples of matrices whose products are [1].

$$[0 \quad 1] \begin{bmatrix} 0 \\ 1 \end{bmatrix} = [1] \qquad [1 \quad 0] \begin{bmatrix} 1 \\ 0 \end{bmatrix} = [1]$$

$$[2 \quad 1 \quad 1] \begin{bmatrix} 2 \\ {}^-2 \\ 1 \end{bmatrix} = [1] \qquad [{}^-3 \quad 13] \begin{bmatrix} 4 \\ 1 \end{bmatrix} = [1]$$

B10 The order of matrix multiplication does matter, in fact one order may not even be possible. For example:

if $\underline{A} = \begin{bmatrix} 1 & 2 \\ 3 & 4 \end{bmatrix}$ and $\underline{B} = \begin{bmatrix} 5 & 6 \\ 7 & 8 \end{bmatrix}$

then $\underline{AB} = \begin{bmatrix} 1 & 2 \\ 3 & 4 \end{bmatrix}\begin{bmatrix} 5 & 6 \\ 7 & 8 \end{bmatrix} = \begin{bmatrix} 19 & 22 \\ 43 & 50 \end{bmatrix}$ and

$\underline{BA} = \begin{bmatrix} 5 & 6 \\ 7 & 8 \end{bmatrix}\begin{bmatrix} 1 & 2 \\ 3 & 4 \end{bmatrix} = \begin{bmatrix} 23 & 34 \\ 31 & 46 \end{bmatrix}$

$\begin{bmatrix} 1 & 3 \\ 1 & 0 \end{bmatrix}\begin{bmatrix} 2 & 2 & 0 \\ 6 & {}^-3 & {}^-2 \end{bmatrix}$ is possible but

$\begin{bmatrix} 2 & 2 & 0 \\ 6 & {}^-3 & {}^-2 \end{bmatrix}\begin{bmatrix} 1 & 3 \\ 1 & 0 \end{bmatrix}$ is not.

B11 (a) $2x + y = 3, x + y = 2$ can be represented by:

$$\begin{bmatrix} 2 & 1 \\ 1 & 1 \\ 3 & 2 \end{bmatrix}$$

Multiply the second column by 2 $\Rightarrow \begin{bmatrix} 2 & 2 \\ 1 & 2 \\ 3 & 4 \end{bmatrix}$

Now subtract the second column from the first $\Rightarrow \begin{bmatrix} 2 & 0 \\ 1 & {}^-1 \\ 3 & {}^-1 \end{bmatrix}$

Add the second column to the first $\Rightarrow \begin{bmatrix} 2 & 0 \\ 0 & {}^-1 \\ 2 & {}^-1 \end{bmatrix}$

So $2x + 0 = 2$ and $0 - y = {}^-1$
$\therefore 2x = 2$, so $x = 1$
$^-y = {}^-1$, so $y = 1$

(b) $2x + 3y = 5, x + y = 1$ can be represented by:

$$\begin{bmatrix} 2 & 1 \\ 3 & 1 \\ 5 & 1 \end{bmatrix}$$

Multiply the second column by 2 $\Rightarrow \begin{bmatrix} 2 & 2 \\ 3 & 2 \\ 5 & 2 \end{bmatrix}$

Now subtract the first column from the second $\Rightarrow \begin{bmatrix} 2 & 0 \\ 3 & {}^-1 \\ 5 & {}^-3 \end{bmatrix}$

Add three times the second column to the first $\Rightarrow \begin{bmatrix} 2 & 0 \\ 0 & {}^-1 \\ {}^-4 & {}^-3 \end{bmatrix}$

So $2x + 0 = {}^-4$ and $0 - y = {}^-3$
$\therefore 2x = {}^-4$, so $x = {}^-2$
$^-y = {}^-3$, so $y = 3$

A zero in the top right-hand corner eliminates x from one of the equations and a zero in the middle row of the left-hand column eliminates y.

Options

Your own spreadsheets and observations

10 Iterative solution of equations

The work in this chapter builds on that already encountered in *Book Y5* new edition, Chapter 12 ('Iteration'). Iterative solution of equations is also covered in SMP 16–19 *Foundations* (Chapter 5). Although the convergence of sequences arises in this chapter, the topic is dealt with more generally in *Book YX2*.

It is assumed throughout this chapter that students are confident in using the subscript notation for sequence terms (i.e. $u_{n+1} = f(u_n)$). A graphical calculator or spreadsheet should, if at all possible, be available to all students.

Section A draws students' attention to the use of iteration to solve linear equations. The aim is to give some justification for the link between u_{n+1}, u_n and x in an equation. Without this, iterative methods tend to become 'magical' operations. Section B looks at the solution of quadratic equations by iteration. Attention is given to the rearrangement of the original equation into the appropriate form. Situations where rearrangement of an equation into the form $u_{n+1} = f(u_n)$ do not give a solution, because the sequences do not converge, are encountered in Section C. Students are invited to solve various polynomials by whatever methods they consider appropriate in Section D. This could provide useful material for discussion.

With many of the questions in this chapter you will need to decide to how many significant figures to give your answers.

A Iterative formulas and equations

A1

	Iterative formula	u_1	u_2	u_3	u_4	u_5	u_6
(a)	$u_{n+1} = u_n + 7$	7	14	21	28	35	42
(b)	$u_{n+1} = \dfrac{u_n}{2} + 1$	2	2	2	2	2	2
(c)	$u_{n+1} = \dfrac{1}{u_n} + 1$	4	1·25	1·8	1·555 555 6	1·642 857 1	1·608 695 7
(d)	$u_{n+1} = \sqrt{(u_n + 7)}$	3	3·162 277 7	3·187 832 8	3·191 838 5	3·192 465 9	3·192 564 2

(e) The sequences in (c) (1·618 033 989) and (d) (3·192 582 404) converge to a limit.

A2 (a) $x = \dfrac{x + 18}{4} \Rightarrow 4x = x + 18 \Rightarrow 3x = 18 \Rightarrow x = 6$

The symbol $\Rightarrow$ means implies, it does a different job from the '=' sign.
(b) The sequence converges to 6 when $u_1 = 10$.
(c) They appear to be the same.

A3 (a) $u_{n+1} = \dfrac{u_n + 8}{3}$

$u_1 = 6,\qquad u_2 = 4\cdot\dot{6},\qquad u_3 = 4\cdot\dot{2},$
$u_4 = 4\cdot07\dot{4},\ u_5 = 4\cdot024\,691\,4,\ u_6 = 4\cdot008\,230\,4$
The sequence seems to converge to 4.
(b) $x = \dfrac{x + 8}{3} \Rightarrow 3x = x + 8 \Rightarrow 2x = 8 \Rightarrow x = 4$
(c) The solution and the limit of the sequence are the same.

A4 (a) The first term in the sequence is 3.
(b) $u_{n+1} = \dfrac{u_n + 20}{2}$
(c) The limit of the sequence appears to be 20.

A5 The sequence seems to converge whatever the value of u_1, including negative values.

A6 $u_{n+1} = \dfrac{2u_n - 3}{5}$

This **tends** to the limit $^-1$, whatever the value of u_1.
You could check this using a BASIC program.

A7

	Equation	Solution	Iterative formula	Solution from limit of formula
(a)	$x = \dfrac{x - 2}{3}$	$x = {}^-1$	$u_{n+1} = \dfrac{u_n - 2}{3}$	Yes
(b)	$x = \dfrac{x + 2}{5}$	$x = \frac{1}{2}$	$u_{n+1} = \dfrac{u_n + 2}{5}$	Yes
(c)	$x = \dfrac{2x - 2}{3}$	$x = {}^-2$	$u_{n+1} = \dfrac{2u_n - 2}{3}$	Yes

Your own observations
Some of the iterative formulas take a long time to converge.

B Iteration and quadratic equations

B1 Substituting $x = 2 \cdot 317$ in $x(x + 2)$ gives $10 \cdot 002\,489$ which is very close to 10. So this value of x is an approximate solution to the equation $x(x + 2) = 10$.

B2 $u_1 = 1$, $u_2 = 1\dot{\cdot}\dot{6}$, $u_3 = 1\dot{\cdot}3\dot{6}$, $u_4 = 1\cdot48\dot{6}$, $u_5 = 1\cdot434\,108\,5$, $u_6 = 1\cdot455\,981\,9$, $u_7 = 1\cdot446\,766\,8$, $u_8 = 1\cdot450\,634\,8$, ...

The limit of the sequence is $1 \cdot 45$ to 2 d.p. Substituting this value for x in the expression $x(x + 2)$ gives $5 \cdot 0025$. So this is one of the solutions to $x(x + 2) = 5$.

B3 (a) is not a correct rearrangement:
$$x = \frac{x^2 - 5}{2} \Rightarrow x^2 - 2x - 5 = 0$$

(b) is a correct rearrangement:
$$x = \frac{x^2 + 2}{5} \Rightarrow x^2 - 5x + 2 = 0$$

(c) is a correct rearrangement:
$$x = 5 - \frac{2}{x} \Rightarrow x^2 = 5x - 2 \Rightarrow x^2 - 5x + 2 = 0$$

(d) is not a correct rearrangement:
$$x = \sqrt{(2 + 5x)} \Rightarrow x^2 = 2 + 5x \Rightarrow x^2 - 5x - 2 = 0$$

B4 (a) The limit of the sequence $u_{n+1} = \dfrac{1}{u_n} + 2$ is $2 \cdot 41$ (to 2 d.p.) when $u_1 = 2$.

(b) $2 \cdot 41^2 - 2(2 \cdot 14) - 1 = {}^-0 \cdot 0119 \approx 0$
Why isn't it exactly zero?

B5 (a) $u_1 = 1$, $u_2 = 0\dot{\cdot}\dot{6}$, $u_3 = 0\cdot432\,098\,8$, $u_4 = 0\cdot360\,225\,6$, $u_5 = 0\cdot348\,914\,6$, $u_6 = 0\cdot347\,492\,4$, ...
The solution is $0 \cdot 35$ to 2 d.p.

(b) $\dfrac{0 \cdot 35^3 + 1}{3} \approx 0 \cdot 35$

B6 (a) $x(x + 3) = 20 \Rightarrow x = \dfrac{20}{x + 3}$

(b) $u_{n+1} = \dfrac{20}{u_n + 3}$

(c) $u_1 = 3$, $u_2 = 3\cdot\dot{3}$, $u_3 = 3\cdot157\,894\,7$, $u_4 = 3\cdot247\,863\,2$, $u_5 = 3\cdot201\,094\,4$, ...
The limit is $3 \cdot 22$ to 2 d.p.

(d) Substituting in $x(x + 3)$ gives the value $20 \cdot 0284 \approx 20$.

B7 The iterative formula is $u_{n+1} = \dfrac{5}{u_n}$.

This has a limit of $1 \cdot 449\,489\,743$ or $1 \cdot 45$ to 2 d.p. The expression $x^2 + 2x - 5$ has a value of $0 \cdot 0025 \approx 0$ when $x = 1 \cdot 45$, so this is one of the solutions.

B8 (a) $x^2 - 3x - 5 = 0 \Rightarrow x(x - 3) = 5 \Rightarrow x = \dfrac{5}{x - 3}$

(b) $u_{n+1} = \dfrac{5}{u_n - 3}$

(c) $u_1 = 5$, $u_2 = 2 \cdot 5$, $u_3 = {}^-10$, $u_4 = {}^-0\cdot384\,61\dot{5}$, $u_5 = {}^-1\cdot477\,2\dot{7}$, $u_6 = {}^-1\cdot116\,751\,3$, $u_7 = {}^-1\cdot214\,549\,9$, $u_8 = {}^-1\cdot186\,366\,3$, $u_9 = {}^-1\cdot194\,353\,2$
The solution is $x = {}^-1 \cdot 19$ to 2 d.p.

(d) Substituting into $x^2 - 3x - 5$ gives ${}^-0 \cdot 0139 \approx 0$.

B9 Your own iterations
Did you manage to find both solutions?

Challenge
$$x^2 + ax + b = 0 \Rightarrow x(x + a) = {}^-b \Rightarrow x = \frac{{}^-b}{x + a}$$

which gives $u_{n+1} = \dfrac{{}^-b}{u_n + a}$

or
$$x^2 + ax + b = 0 \Rightarrow ax = {}^-x^2 - b \Rightarrow x = \frac{{}^-x^2 - b}{a}$$

which gives $u_{n+1} = \dfrac{{}^-u_n{}^2 - b}{a}$

Do both iterative equations give the same solutions?

C Bugs

C1 (a) $x^2 + x - 5 = 0 \Rightarrow x = 5 - x^2$

(b) The iterative formula $u_{n+1} = 5 - u_n{}^2$ **diverges** whatever value of u_1 is chosen.
So it cannot be used to solve $x^2 + x - 5 = 0$.

C2 [a] $u_{n+1} = \dfrac{15}{u_n + 2}$ [b] $u_{n+1} = \dfrac{15 - u_n{}^2}{2}$

[c] $u_{n+1} = \sqrt{(15 - 2u_n)}$

(a) Probably one of the easiest ways to investigate these iterative formulas for convergence is to use a spreadsheet to trial a range of values for u_1. Here is one way – you may have a better one!

	A	B	C	D	E
1	U1 =	−3.5	Un+1 = 15/(Un+2)	Un+1 = (15 − Un^2)/2	Un+1 = (15 − 2Un)^0.5
2			=$B$1	=$B$1	=$B$1
3			=15/(C2+2)	=(15−D2^2)/2	=(15−2*E2)^0.5
4			=15/(C3+2)	=(15−D3^2)/2	=(15−2*E3)^0.5

It looks as if the iterative formulas [a] and [c] converge (to a value of 3), but [b] doesn't. With some starting values, over 50 iterations may be needed in order to be reasonably sure that the sequence is converging. Formula [b] only converges on 3 with a starting value of 3.

(b) The iterative formulas [a] and [c] both give a solution of 3.

(c) $x^2 + 2x - 15 = (x + 5)(x - 3) = 0$, so one of the solutions is $x = 3$, but the other ($x = {}^-5$) is not possible to find using the iterative formulas here.

C3 (a) Using $u_{n+1} = \dfrac{4}{u_n + 1}$ gives the solution $1 \cdot 56$ (to 2 d.p.). In other words it only gives one solution.

(b) $x^2 + x - 4 = 0 \Rightarrow x(x + 1) = 4 \Rightarrow x + 1 = \dfrac{4}{x}$
$$\Rightarrow x = \frac{4}{x} - 1$$

(c) Using $u_{n+1} = \dfrac{4}{u_n} - 1$ gives the solution ${}^-2 \cdot 56$ (to 2 d.p.) – the second solution.

C4 $x^2 - 10x + 3 = 0 \Rightarrow 10x = x^2 + 3 \Rightarrow x = \dfrac{x^2 + 3}{10}$

(so $a = 3$ and $b = 10$)

Investigating $u_{n+1} = \dfrac{u_n^2 + 3}{10}$:

(a) When $u_1 = 0$ the sequence converges to 0·31 (to 2 d.p.).

(b) When $u_1 = 5$ the sequence converges to 0·31 (to 2 d.p.).

(c) When $u_1 = 10$ the sequence diverges.

One root of $x^2 - 10x + 3 = 0$ to 2 d.p. is 0·31. You can easily check this value by substituting back into the equation.

C5 The iterative formulas $u_{n+1} = \dfrac{5}{u_n + 2}$ and $u_{n+1} = \sqrt{(5 - 2u_n)}$ both converge to 1·45 (to 2 d.p.).

The iterative formula $u_{n+1} = \dfrac{5 - u_n^2}{2}$ does not converge, even after a very large number of iterations.

One solution to $x(x + 2) = 5$ is 1·45 (to 2 d.p.). It is not possible to find the other solution by iteration, even for values of u_1 round about ⁻3·5.

C6

U1=	2	Un+1=(10/Un)^0.5	Un+1 = 10/(Un^2)	Un+1=((10Un)^0.5)^0.5
Iteration no.		2.23606797749979	2.5	2.11474252688113
2		2.11474252688113	1.6	2.14444234668776
3		2.17455927604098	3.90625	2.15193224757471
4		2.14444234668776	0.65536	2.153808880673304
57		2.15443469003188	*Error*	2.15443469003188
58		2.15443469003188	0	2.15443469003188
59		2.15443469003188	*Error*	2.15443469003188
60		2.15443469003188	0	2.15443469003188
61		2.15443469003188	*Error*	2.15443469003188
62		2.15443469003188	0	2.15443469003188

What is the error in the second iteration?

According to the results above $x = 2·15$ (to 2 d.p.) is a solution to $x^3 = 10$ (check $2·15^3 \approx 10$).

D Take your pick

For this section you will have chosen your own method for each question. You may have used a different method from that given in the answer.

D1 Iterative methods do not seem to work here. Drawing the graph of $y = x^3 + 2x - 7$ and finding where it cuts the x-axis seems to be the best method, especially if a graph-plotter is available. The solution, to 1 d.p, is 1·6 – judging by the graph this is the only solution.

D2 This can be solved by factorising. The solutions are $x = 3$ and $x = ⁻1$.

D3 Let x be the number: $7x = 1 + \dfrac{1}{x}$. This gives the iterative formula $u_{n+1} = \dfrac{1}{7}(1 + \dfrac{1}{u_n})$, which gives $x = 0·46$ as a solution. It can also be quite easily solved by trial and improvement.

D4 Plotting $y = x^3 - 3x$ and finding the x-coordinates of the point(s) where it cuts the x-axis seems to be the most straightforward method. There are three solutions: $x = 0$, $x = 1·73$ and $x = ⁻1·73$. Trial and improvement is also easy to use here.

D5 The equation which needs to be solved is $50(\phi - \sin \phi) = 100$ or $\phi - \sin \phi = 2$. Finding where $y = x - \sin x - 2$ cuts the x-axis is one method – providing you remember to work in radians! Iteration can also be used: $u_{n+1} = 2 + \sin u_n$. Both methods give a solution of 2·55^c. This is equal to 146° (to the nearest degree).

D6 You need to remember to work in radians. Using the iterative formula $u_{n+1} = 3(\cos u_n + 1)$ seems a possibility. However, it does not converge but oscillates between 0 and 6. The next approach is to use a graphical method, for example finding where $y = x$ intersects $y = 3(\cos x + 1)$ or, more easily, where $y = 3(\cos x + 1) - x$ cuts the x-axis. There is one solution between 0 and 2π at $x = 1·94^c$ (to 2 d.p.).

D7 This can be solved using either radians or degrees. The solution is best found by finding $\cos^{-1} 0·5$. The solutions between 0° and 360° are 60° and 300° (1·05^c and 5·24^c).

D8 The formula gives

$$x = \sqrt[3]{\left(\dfrac{-4}{2} + \sqrt{\dfrac{4^2}{4} + \dfrac{-3^3}{27}}\right)} - \sqrt[3]{\left(\dfrac{-4}{2} - \sqrt{\left(\dfrac{4^2}{4} + \dfrac{-3^3}{27}\right)}\right)}$$

(Remember $\sqrt[3]{8}$ means the cube root of 8.) So $x = \sqrt[3]{(-2 + \sqrt{3})} - \sqrt[3]{(2 + \sqrt{3})} = ⁻2·20$ (to 2 d.p.)

D9 One method to solve $x^2 - 10x + 3 = 0$ is to use the formula on page 54. ($b = ⁻10$ and $c = 3$ in $x = ⁻\frac{1}{2}b \pm \sqrt{(\frac{1}{4}b^2 - c)}$) The solutions are $5 \pm \sqrt{(25 - 3)} = 5 \pm \sqrt{22}$. So $x = 9·690$ or $x = 0·310$.

Mixed bag 3

1 Your own results and conclusions
The mean life spans would probably not be too helpful in this situation. A useful approach would be to compare the percentage cumulative frequencies of the life spans for Egyptians with present day people. Details of present day figures will need a trip to the library or you could ask your Geography teacher. (Remember you did some work involving cumulative percentages in *Book Y3*, Chapter 17.)

You may need to combine male and female figures. In fact the sample of Egyptians is biased – only the very rich could afford to be mummified.

2 The graph $y = \sin x$ (x measured in degrees) repeats itself after 360° – this is its cycle length. This means that $\sin(360 + x)$ has the same value as $\sin x$. So the sine of any multiple of 360° added to an angle is simply the sine of that angle. (*Experiment with a calculator if you're not convinced!*)
Put into symbols, this means that
$\sin(x + 360n) = \sin x = z$ so $\sin^{-1} z = x$, where n is a whole number. 1980 is a multiple of 360 so adding it to your age, finding the sine of the result and then finally finding the inverse sine of this will simply give you back your age.
Will it work for people born after 1980 – with negative ages? Is there a similar effect for other trigonometric functions?

3 The area of a circle diameter d is $\pi \dfrac{d^2}{4}$. The Egyptian expression was $\left(d - \dfrac{d}{9}\right)^2$ which is $\left(\dfrac{8d}{9}\right)^2$ or $\dfrac{64}{81}d^2$.
Equating these expressions for the area of a circle gives $\pi \dfrac{d^2}{4} = \dfrac{64}{81}d^2$.
This implies a value of the 'Egyptian π' of $\dfrac{4 \times 64}{81} \approx 3{\cdot}16$ – a good approximation.

4

×	$(x + 1)$	$(x + 3)$	$(x + 5)$
$(x - 1)$	$x^2 - 1$	$x^2 + 2x - 3$	$x^2 + 4x - 5$
$(x + 4)$	$x^2 + 5x + 4$	$x^2 + 7x + 12$	$x^2 + 9x + 20$
$(x - 5)$	$x^2 - 4x - 5$	$x^2 - 2x - 15$	$x^2 - 25$

5 Division by zero is not allowed – where is this rule broken?

6 With problems like this it is best to list all the outcomes systematically. Label the counters a and b. Counter a can be red (R_a) or blue (B_a) while counter b is red (R_b).

Counter taken out	Counter left in bag
R_a	R_b
B_a	R_b
R_b	R_a
R_b	B_a

So the probability that the counter left in the bag is red is $\frac{3}{4}$.

7 Let x be the number of days the carpenter worked. Over the 30 days he earned $2x$ francs but forfeited $3(30 - x)$ francs.
$2x = 3(30 - x)$, so $x = 18$ days

8 (a) For n cities the number of roads needed so that each city is linked to every other city is $\dfrac{n}{2}(n - 1)$.
Can you work out why this formula is correct?
So for five cities 10 roads are needed.

(b) There is also a formula for the least number of flyovers needed (you probably found your answer by actually counting). For n cities the number is
$\dfrac{n(n - 2)^2(n - 4)}{64}$ if n is even,
and $\dfrac{(n - 1)^2(n - 3)^2}{64}$ if n is odd.
So for five cities just 1 flyover is necessary.

9 You could investigate this by drawing the graphs of $y = x$ and $y = \dfrac{1}{x}$.
$x > \dfrac{1}{x}$ for $x > 1$ and for $^-1 < x < 0$

Review questions

1 Angles and circles 1

1.1 *You must give reasons for each step in your working.*
(a) $a = 100°, b = 40°$ (b) $a = 90°, b = 25°$
(c) $a = 70°, b = 15°$ (d) $a = 105°$
(e) $a = 130°, b = 150°$ (f) $a = 20°, b = 70°$

1.2 $\angle ABC = 130°, \angle DCB = 60°$

1.3 (a) $\angle DBA = 60°$ (b) $\angle DAB = 90°$
(c) $\angle DBC = 40°$ (d) $\angle ADB = 30°$

2 Rational and irrational numbers

2.1 (a) $\frac{15}{99} (= \frac{5}{33})$ (b) $\frac{311}{990}$ ($99x = 31\cdot1 \Rightarrow x = \frac{311}{990}$)
(c) $\frac{2}{9}$ (d) $\frac{284}{999}$

2.2 (a) (i) $6 (= 2 \times 3)$ and $35 (= 5 \times 7)$ are co-prime.
      (ii) $18 (= 2 \times 3 \times 3)$ and 19 are co-prime.
      (iii) $42 (= 2 \times 3 \times 7)$ and $77 (= 7 \times 11)$ are not co-prime.
      (iv) $36 (= 2 \times 2 \times 3 \times 3)$ and $108 (= 2 \times 2 \times 3 \times 3 \times 3)$ are not co-prime.

(b) For your own set of values of a and b you should have found that $\frac{a}{b}$ gives a recurring decimal.

(c) If x is co-prime with 10 then you should have found that $\frac{1}{x}$ gives a pure recurring decimal.

Continue this table for recurring decimals formed from $\frac{1}{x}$.

Number x	Pure recurring decimal $\frac{1}{x}$	Impure recurring decimal $\frac{1}{x}$	Prime factors of x
3	✓		
6		✓	2, 3
7	✓		
9	✓		3

2.3 A decimal which is terminating or recurring can be written in the form of a fraction. Any number which can be written exactly as a fraction can be written as a decimal (either recurring or terminating).

2.4 (a) The last digit in the square of a whole number must be one of these:
    0   1   4   5   6   9

(b) The last digit of an integer squared multiplied by 8 can only be:
    0   2   8
So it cannot be any of these digits:
    1   3   4   5   6   7   9

(c) Assume that $\sqrt{68}$ is rational, so it can be written as a fraction, say $\frac{a}{b}$ (and assume that the fraction is in its simplest form).
This means that $68 = \frac{a^2}{b^2}$ or $68b^2 = a^2$.
$68b^2$ can only end with a 0, 2 or 8.
But a^2 can only end in 0, 1, 4, 5, 6 or 9. But the last digits of $68b^2$ and a^2 cannot both be zero. *Why not?*
So the initial assumption must be false.
Therefore $\sqrt{68}$ is an irrational number.

2.5 (a) $\sqrt{16} = 4$, which is rational.
(b) $\sqrt{18}$ is irrational (see answer to **2.4**).
(c) π is irrational.
(d) $0\cdot\dot{5} = \frac{5}{9}$, so it is rational.
(e) $0\cdot110\,110\,011\,000\,110\,000\,11 \ldots$ is irrational. Although you might confuse it with a recurring decimal, if you look carefully you will see that the pattern does not repeat – the number of zeros is increasing.

2.6 (a) $(\sqrt{3} + 2) + (2 - \sqrt{3}) = 4$, so it is rational.
(b) $(\sqrt{3} + 2)(2 - \sqrt{3}) = 3 + 4 + 2\sqrt{3} - 2\sqrt{3} = 7$, so it is rational.
(c) $\sqrt{\frac{9}{16}} = \frac{3}{4}$, so it is rational.
(d) $\sqrt{3}(\sqrt{12} + \sqrt{27}) = \sqrt{36} + \sqrt{81} = 6 + 9 = 15$, so it is rational.
(e) $\sqrt{(2 + 14)} = \sqrt{16} = 4$, which is rational.
(f) $\sqrt{2} + \sqrt{14}$ cannot be expressed as a rational number; it is irrational.

2.7 (a) $7x - 2 = 15 \Rightarrow x = \frac{17}{7}$, a rational number
(b) $2x - \sqrt{3} = \sqrt{6} \Rightarrow x = \frac{\sqrt{3} + \sqrt{6}}{2}$, an irrational number
(c) $\sqrt{(4x^2)} = 25 \Rightarrow 4x^2 = 625 \Rightarrow x^2 = \frac{625}{4} \Rightarrow x = \frac{25}{2}$, a rational number
(d) $x^2 - 1 = 3 \Rightarrow x = \sqrt{4} = 2$, a rational number
(e) $\sqrt{x} - 1 = 3 \Rightarrow x = 16$, a rational number
(f) $x^2 - 1 = 2 \Rightarrow x^2 = 3 \Rightarrow x = \sqrt{3}$, an irrational number

3 Tangents and curves

3.1 Cooling rate $= \dfrac{500 - 400}{100 \times 24 \times 60 \times 60} \approx 0\cdot000\,012$ or $1\cdot2 \times 10^{-5}°C/s$

3.2 Your answers may be slightly different to these.

(a)
Graph showing height of the rocket against time after launching

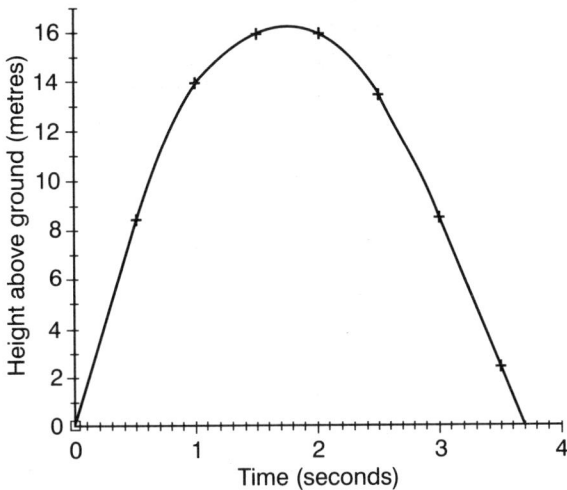

(b) The rocket's speed 1 second after launching is the gradient of the curve at this time ≈ 7 m/s.

(c) The maximum speed will be at the point where the gradient is greatest. This is at take-off and is about 17 m/s.

(d) The rocket's speed on impact is given by the gradient at zero height. This is about 15 m/s.

3.3 The car accelerates rapidly at first, then the acceleration lessens. The car then starts to decelerate (i.e. negative acceleration) slowly, increasing to a maximum deceleration before decelerating less and less. The maximum deceleration is approximately equal in magnitude to the initial acceleration.

3.4 (a) It helps if the height axis is broken, i.e. does not start at 0.

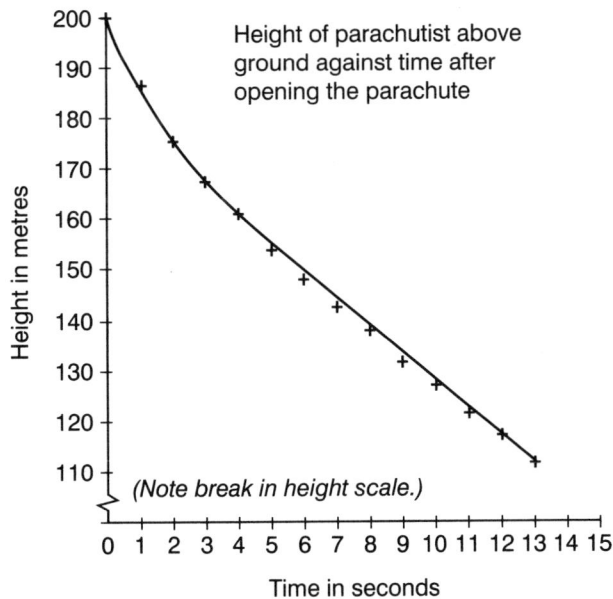

Height of parachutist above ground against time after opening the parachute

(Note break in height scale.)

(b) After 2 seconds the velocity is approximately 10 m/s, and after 4 seconds it is approximately 7 m/s. But after about 5 seconds the velocity of the parachutist settles down to a constant value of about 5 m/s.

(c) After about 15 seconds the parachutist is 100 metres above the ground. As she is falling with a velocity of 5 m/s the final 100 metres will take 20 seconds. So the total time to reach the ground from the parachute opening is 35 seconds.

(d) As the gradient is changing rapidly, you should also plot the velocity at 1 second. Remember that the velocity at $t = 0$ is 50 m/s. The parachutist has a very large acceleration (over 40 m/s^2) when she opens her parachute. This then decreases until it reaches zero after about 5 seconds. Thereafter she has zero acceleration.
(Unless your parachute is very large, we would recommend that you open it before you reach 200 m!)

4 Compounding errors

4.1 (a) 38 m to 42 m (b) 57·9 °C to 58·1 °C
(c) 670·6 km/hour to 671·4 km/hour

4.2 (a) 199 km to 201 km
(b) 17·1 km/hour to 18·9 km/hour
(c) 28 ohms to 42 ohms
(d) 10·29 s to 10·71 s (or 10·3 to 10·7)

4.3 Taking $\pi = 3\cdot142$:

maximum volume of cylinder
$$= \pi \frac{10\cdot5^2}{4} \times 20\cdot5 \text{ cm}^3 \approx 1775 \text{ cm}^3$$

minimum volume of cylinder
$$= \pi \frac{9\cdot5^2}{4} \times 19\cdot5 \text{ cm}^3 \approx 1382 \text{ cm}^3$$

4.4 Least area of cross-section $= 19$ cm^2
least height $= 9$ cm
So least possible volume $= 19 \times 9 = 171$ cm^3

4.5 The answer given is only approximate. Your answer and method may be different from those here.
The accuracy of the speed needs to be about $\pm\, 0\cdot0002\%$ (0·001 m.p.h. in 650 m.p.h.).
This working assumes that the relative uncertainty needs to be about the same for the distance and time measurements. In actual fact it is more accurate to say that they must each be half of this figure.
The mile must be measured to 0·0002%, which is about 0·1 of an inch (a mile is 5280 feet, there are 12 inches in a foot).
To travel 1 mile at about 650 m.p.h. takes 5·5 seconds, so the time needs to be measured to about 0·000 01 s.

4.6 (a) e can vary between $6.75°$ and $7.25°$.
d can vary between 1188 m and 1212 m.
h is given by $h = d\tan e$,
so h can vary between 140·61 m and 154·19 m,
which can be written as 147.4 ± 6.8 m.
This is a relative error of about 5%.

(b) For a cloud height of about 150 m, if there
were no errors in the time or speed
measurements, the balloon would take about
3 minutes to disappear.
The uncertainty in the timing is 1 second,
which is a relative error of about $\pm 0.5\%$. This
is small compared with the relative error in
the balloon speed ($\pm 5\%$), so a figure of $\pm 5\%$
can be taken as a good approximation for the
relative error in the cloud height. So the two
methods have about the same relative error.

5 Using graphs to solve equations

5.1 *Don't forget that all the angles are in radians.*

(a) $x = 1.4^c$ and 4.8^c
(x-coordinates of the intersection of
$y = 4\cos x$ and $y = 0.5$)

(b) $x = 1.4^c$ and 5.2^c
(x-coordinates of the intersection of
$y = 4\cos x$ and $y = \dfrac{x}{3}$)

(c) $x = 1.4^c$ and 5.2^c
(rearrangement gives the same equation as (b))

5.2 The equation to be solved is $9.38(d^2 + 2.25d) = 30$.
One way is to find where $y = 9.38(d^2 + 2.25d) - 30$
cuts the d-axis.
A thickness to the nearest 0.1 or 0.01 of an inch
should be accurate enough. The solution is 0.998,
or 1.00 inch to 2 d.p.

5.3 Here are the solutions to $x^2 + x = c$ for various
values of c.

Value of c	Roots of the equation $x^2 + x = c$	
0	0.00	⁻1.00
1	0.62	⁻1.62
2	1.00	⁻2.00
3	1.30	⁻2.30
4	1.56	⁻2.56
5	1.79	⁻2.79
6	2.00	⁻3.00
7	2.19	⁻3.19
8	2.37	⁻3.37
9	2.54	⁻3.54
10	2.70	⁻3.70
11	2.85	⁻3.85
12	3.00	⁻4.00
13	3.14	⁻4.14

From these results it can be seen that the sum of
the roots in each equation is always ⁻1. Careful
inspection of the table also shows that the product
of the two roots is ⁻c.

Challenge
*Can you prove the observations in **5.3** using the
expression for the roots of a quadratic equation?*

5.4 (a) $x = 0.55$ and $x = 5.43$
(b) $x = ⁻0.19$ and $x = 5.19$

5.5 The equation to be solved is $\dfrac{1000t^2}{t^2 + 1} = 500$. Plotting
the graph of $\dfrac{1000t^2}{t^2 + 1}$ against t would give the
solution, but it is sometimes a good idea to look at
the equation before doing anything. This is very
true here, because just by trying $t = 1$ the
equation is solved.
However, the graph is useful in showing how the
disease progresses. A lot of people catch it in the
first few weeks, then the number of fresh cases gets
less and less. The total number who have caught
the disease gets closer and closer to 1000. This is
probably the population of the community.

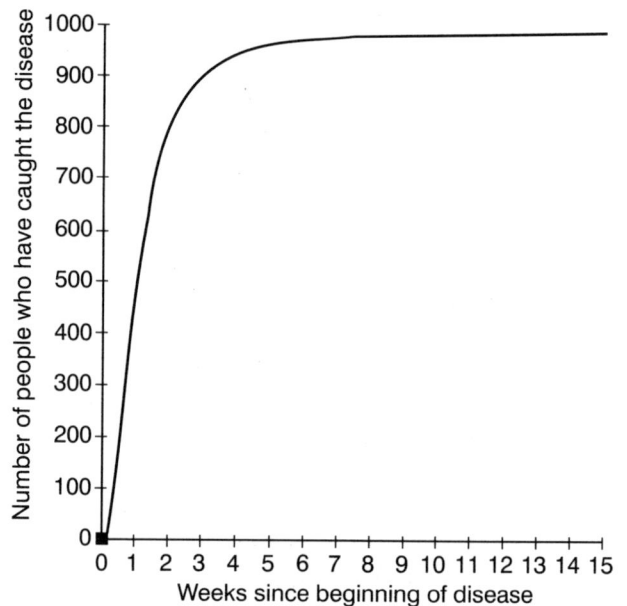

*Investigate the effect of altering the '1' in the
denominator of $\dfrac{1000t^2}{t^2 + 1}$.*

5.6 A graph plotter comes in very useful here.

Light intensity

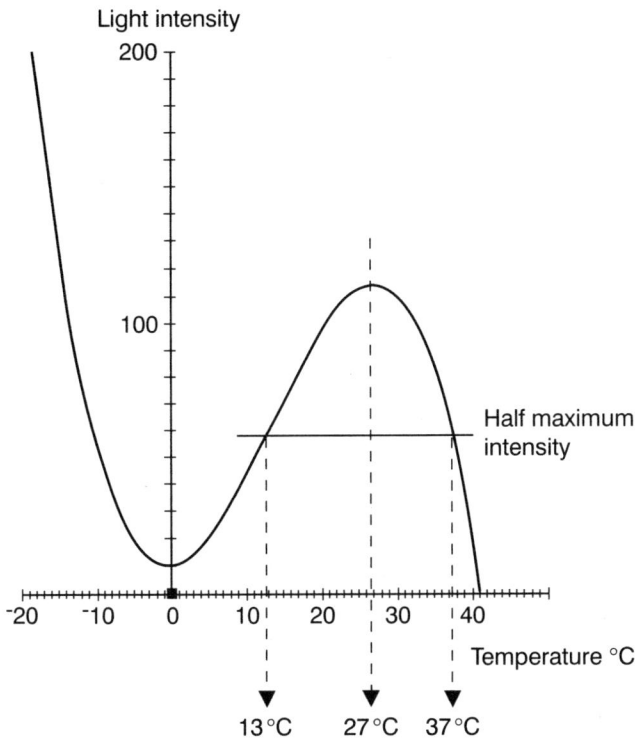

(a) The temperature of maximum light intensity is 27 °C.

(b) The two temperatures at which the brightness is half the maximum are 13 °C and 37 °C. The lower temperature seems a little too low for fireflies!

6 Congruency

6.1 (a) Congruent (SAS)
(b) Not congruent
(c) Not necessarily congruent (*Why not?*)
(d) Not necessarily congruent
(e) Congruent (ASA)

6.2 As the two triangles have equal corresponding angles they must be similar. They have equal areas (scale factor of 1) so they must be congruent.

6.3

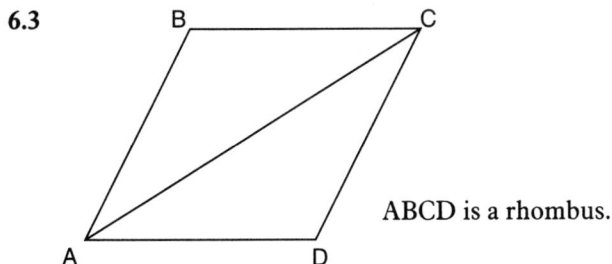

ABCD is a rhombus.

In $\triangle$ABC and $\triangle$ADC:
    AB = CD   (all sides of a rhombus are equal)
    BC = AD   (all sides of a rhombus are equal)
    AC is common to both triangles.
So $\triangle$ABC and $\triangle$ADC are congruent (SSS).
$\therefore \angle$CAB = $\angle$CAD   (corresponding angles in congruent triangles)
Similarly, $\angle$BCA = $\angle$DCA
So AC bisects $\angle$BAD and $\angle$BCD.

6.4 $\triangle$BAX is congruent to $\triangle$EDY (RHS).
$\triangle$ACX is congruent to $\triangle$DFY (RHS).
So BX = EY and XC = YF   (corresponding sides of congruent triangles)
$\therefore$ BC (= BX + XC) = EF (= EY + YF)
In triangles ABC and DEF:
    AB = DE and AC = DF   (both given)
    BC = EF   (proved above)
$\therefore$ $\triangle$ABC and $\triangle$DEF are congruent (SSS).

6.5

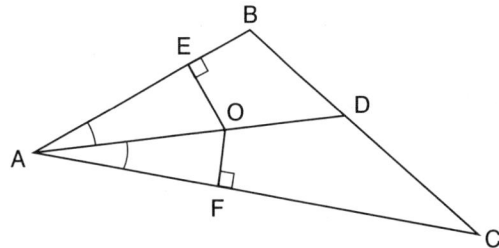

In $\triangle$AEO and $\triangle$AFO:
    $\angle$OAF = $\angle$OAE   (AD bisects $\angle$BAC)
    $\angle$EOA = $\angle$FOA   ($\triangle$AEO and $\triangle$AFO are right-angled)
    AO is common to both triangles.
So $\triangle$AEO and $\triangle$AFO are congruent (ASA).
$\therefore$ OF = OE   (corresponding sides of congruent triangles)

6.6 (a) In $\triangle$ABC and $\triangle$FEA:
    $\angle$AFE = $\angle$CAB   (both right-angles)
    $\angle$FEA = $\angle$EAC   (alternate angles, AC parallel to FE)
    $\therefore$ $\angle$ACB = $\angle$FAE   (angle sum in right-angled triangle)
    $\angle$ABC = $\angle$FEA   (angle sum)
    AE = BC   (given)
So $\triangle$ABC and $\triangle$FEA are congruent (ASA).
You might have written a slightly different proof.

(b) Area of $\triangle$ABE + area of $\triangle$ACE = area of ABEC
In $\triangle$ABE take AB as the base and FE as the height and in $\triangle$ACE take AC as the base and AF as the height.
So $\frac{1}{2}$AB $\times$ FE + $\frac{1}{2}$AC $\times$ AF = $\frac{1}{2}$BC $\times$ AE
But FE = AB and AC = AF   (corresponding sides of congruent triangles FEA and ABC)
So $\frac{1}{2}$AB $\times$ AB + $\frac{1}{2}$AC $\times$ AC = $\frac{1}{2}$BC $\times$ BC
or $AB^2 + AC^2 = BC^2$, which is Pythagoras' rule for $\triangle$ABC.

7 Good fit?

7.1 (a) → C (b) → E (c) → F (d) → D
(e) → C (f) → B (g) → A (h) → F ($y \propto \sqrt{x}$)

7.2 If $a = rb$ and $b = sc^2$ (r and s are constants),
$a = rsc^2$ or $a \propto c^2$.

7.3 Your own explanations for and examples of:
(a) d is directly proportional to e^2.
(b) e is directly proportional to the square root of f.
(c) y is directly proportional to the square of the reciprocal of z (or inversely proportional to z^2).

7.4 One way to choose between Janine's and Abigail's relationships is to plot (a) deflection against length cubed and (b) deflection against length squared. Whichever gives the 'better straight line' after this is the more likely relationship.

Plotting the two graphs shows that the first graph gives a very poor fit to a straight line, whereas the second gives a much better fit.
By finding the gradient of the straight line the relationship between deflection (d mm) and overhang (l mm) is $d = 0 \cdot 0005 l^3$.

8 Angles and circles 2

8.1 (a) $a = 58°, b = 58°$
(b) $a = 40°, b = 50°, c = 40°, d = 10°$
(c) $a = 40°, b = 70°, c = 70°, d = 110°, e = 40°, f = 30°$

8.2 CB = AB (tangents from a point to a circle)
OA = BC (given)
OA = OC (radii of circle)
So all the sides of ABCO are equal.
$\angle$OCB = 90° and $\angle$OAB = 90° (angle between tangent and radius)
∴ ABCO is a square.

8.3 With careful drawing (and within experimental error) you should find that the lines AB and CD are of equal length.
It does not depend on the distance apart of the circles.

8.4 $\angle$CTD (a) = 50° (angle in alternate segment)
$\angle$ATC = 90° (angle subtended by a diameter)
$\angle$ACT = 180° − 90° − 50° = 40° (angle sum of triangle)
∴ $\angle$TCD (b) = 180° − 40° = 140° (angle sum on a straight line)
a, b and c must sum to 180°,
but $a + b = 50° + 140° = 190°$ which is impossible!
The figure is impossible – *you may be able to find some other inconsistencies in the angles.*

9 Introduction to matrices

9.1 Your own explanation as to how to multiply two 2 by 2 matrices.

$$\begin{bmatrix} 1 & 2 \\ 0 & 3 \end{bmatrix}\begin{bmatrix} 0 & 1 \\ 2 & 2 \end{bmatrix} = \begin{bmatrix} 1 \times 0 + 2 \times 2 & 1 \times 1 + 2 \times 2 \\ 0 \times 0 + 3 \times 2 & 0 \times 1 + 3 \times 2 \end{bmatrix}$$

$$= \begin{bmatrix} 4 & 5 \\ 6 & 6 \end{bmatrix}$$

$$\begin{bmatrix} 0 & 1 \\ 2 & 2 \end{bmatrix}\begin{bmatrix} 1 & 2 \\ 0 & 3 \end{bmatrix} = \begin{bmatrix} 0 \times 1 + 1 \times 3 & 0 \times 1 + 1 \times 3 \\ 2 \times 1 + 2 \times 0 & 2 \times 2 + 2 \times 3 \end{bmatrix}$$

$$= \begin{bmatrix} 3 & 3 \\ 2 & 10 \end{bmatrix}$$

The order of multiplication usually makes a difference to the answer – in some cases one multiplication may not even be possible.

9.2 (a) $2\begin{bmatrix} 1 & -1 \\ 0 & 2 \end{bmatrix} = \begin{bmatrix} 2 & -2 \\ 0 & 4 \end{bmatrix}$

(b) $\begin{bmatrix} 1 & -1 \\ 0 & 2 \end{bmatrix} + \begin{bmatrix} 3 & 0 \\ 0 & 1 \\ 2 & 1 \end{bmatrix}$ not possible

(c) $\begin{bmatrix} 1 & -1 \\ 0 & 2 \end{bmatrix}\begin{bmatrix} 1 & -1 \\ 0 & 2 \end{bmatrix} = \begin{bmatrix} 1 & -3 \\ 0 & 4 \end{bmatrix}$

(d) $\begin{bmatrix} 3 & 0 \\ 0 & 1 \\ 2 & 1 \end{bmatrix}\begin{bmatrix} 1 & -1 \\ 0 & 2 \end{bmatrix} = \begin{bmatrix} 3 & -3 \\ 0 & 2 \\ 2 & 0 \end{bmatrix}$

(e) $\begin{bmatrix} 1 & -1 \\ 0 & 2 \end{bmatrix}\begin{bmatrix} -1 & 0 \\ 2 & 1 \end{bmatrix} = \begin{bmatrix} -3 & -1 \\ 4 & 2 \end{bmatrix}$

(f) $\begin{bmatrix} -1 & 0 \\ 2 & 1 \end{bmatrix}\begin{bmatrix} 1 & -1 \\ 0 & 2 \end{bmatrix} = \begin{bmatrix} -1 & 1 \\ 2 & 0 \end{bmatrix}$

(g) $\begin{bmatrix} 1 & -1 \\ 0 & 2 \end{bmatrix}\begin{bmatrix} 3 & 0 \\ 0 & 1 \\ 2 & 1 \end{bmatrix}$ not possible

(h) $\begin{bmatrix} 1 & -1 \\ 0 & 2 \end{bmatrix} - \begin{bmatrix} -1 & 0 \\ 2 & 1 \end{bmatrix} = \begin{bmatrix} 2 & -1 \\ -2 & 1 \end{bmatrix}$

9.3 Your own two matrices whose product is a 3 × 2 matrix and the actual result of the product. (*You could check your answers with a suitable calculator or piece of software.*)

10 Iterative solution of equations

10.1 This question is best done using a spreadsheet.
    (a) Converges to 2·73
    (b) Oscillates between 2 and 5
    (c) Diverges (hence 'error')
    (d) Converges to 0·44

10.2 $x = 1·45$ to 2 d.p.

10.3 (a) $x^2 = 10$
    (b) $x^2 - 5x + 2 = 0$
    (c) $x^2 - 2x - 2 = 0$
    (d) $x^2 - x - 3 = 0$ (square each side)

10.4

	Equation	Iterative formula	Iterative formula	Iterative formula
(a)	$x^2 - 2x - 3 = 0$	$u_{n+1} = \dfrac{u_n{}^2 - 3}{2}$ (generally does not converge)	$u_{n+1} = \dfrac{3}{u_n - 2}$ (converges to $^-1$)	$u_{n+1} = \sqrt{(2u_n + 3)}$ (converges to 3)
(b)	$x^2 - 3 = 0$	$u_{n+1} = \dfrac{3}{u_n}$ (does not converge)	not suitable for solution by iteration	
(c)	$x^2 - 7x = 3$	$u_{n+1} = \dfrac{3}{u_n - 7}$ (converges to $^-0·41$)	$u_{n+1} = \sqrt{(7u_n + 3)}$ (converges to 7·41)	
(d)	$x^2 = x + 4$	$u_{n+1} = \dfrac{4}{u_n - 1}$ (converges to $^-1·56$)	$u_{n+1} = \sqrt{(u_n + 4)}$ (converges to 2·56)	

10.5 You should have worked in radians.
    The answer is $0·20^c$ to 2 d.p.

B6 Rearrange the statements and reasons to show that
$\angle AOB = 2(\angle APB)$. You may find it easier to cut them out.

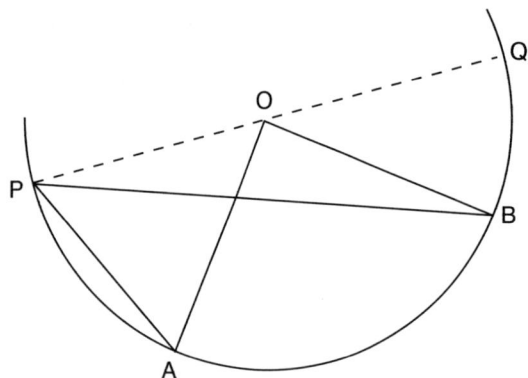

Statement	Reason
$\therefore \angle AOB = 2(\angle APB)$	$\triangle POB$ *is isosceles*
So $\angle POA = 180° - 2x$	*Angles in a triangle sum to 180°*
$\angle OPB = \angle OBP$	*Sides OP and OB are radii of a circle*
$\triangle POA$ is isosceles	*Angles in a triangle sum to 180°*
Let $\angle OPA = x$	*Sides OP and OA are radii of a circle*
So $\angle AOB = (180° - 2y) - (180° - 2x)$	$\triangle POA$ *is isosceles*
$\angle AOB = \angle POB - \angle POA$	
But $\angle APB = x - y$	
Let $\angle OPB = y$	
So $\angle POB = 180° - 2y$	
$\angle AOB = 2(x - y)$	
$\triangle POB$ is isosceles	
$\angle OPA = \angle OAP$	

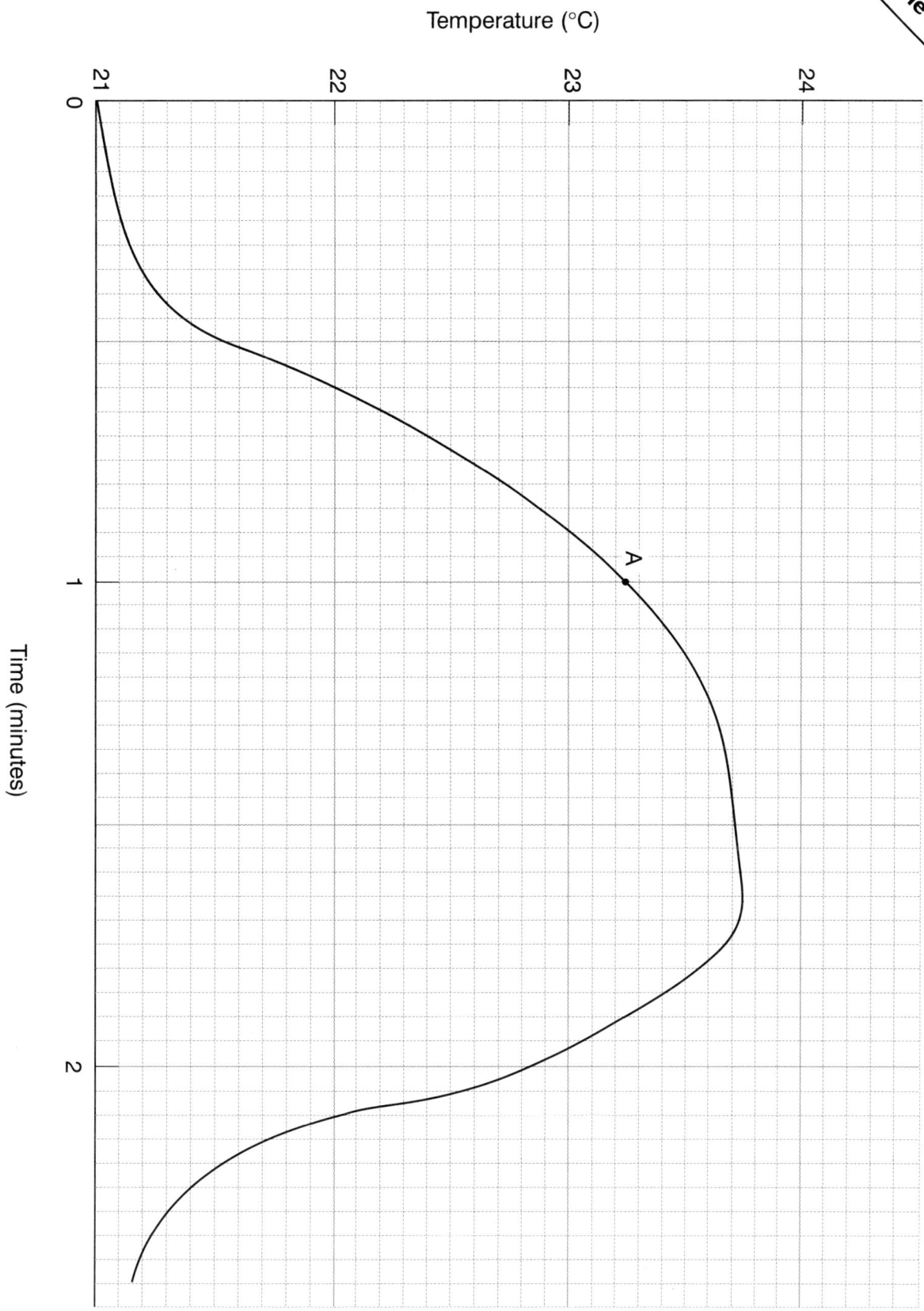

Temperature (°C)

21

22

23

24

A

0

1

2

Time (minutes)

© Cambridge University Press 1995

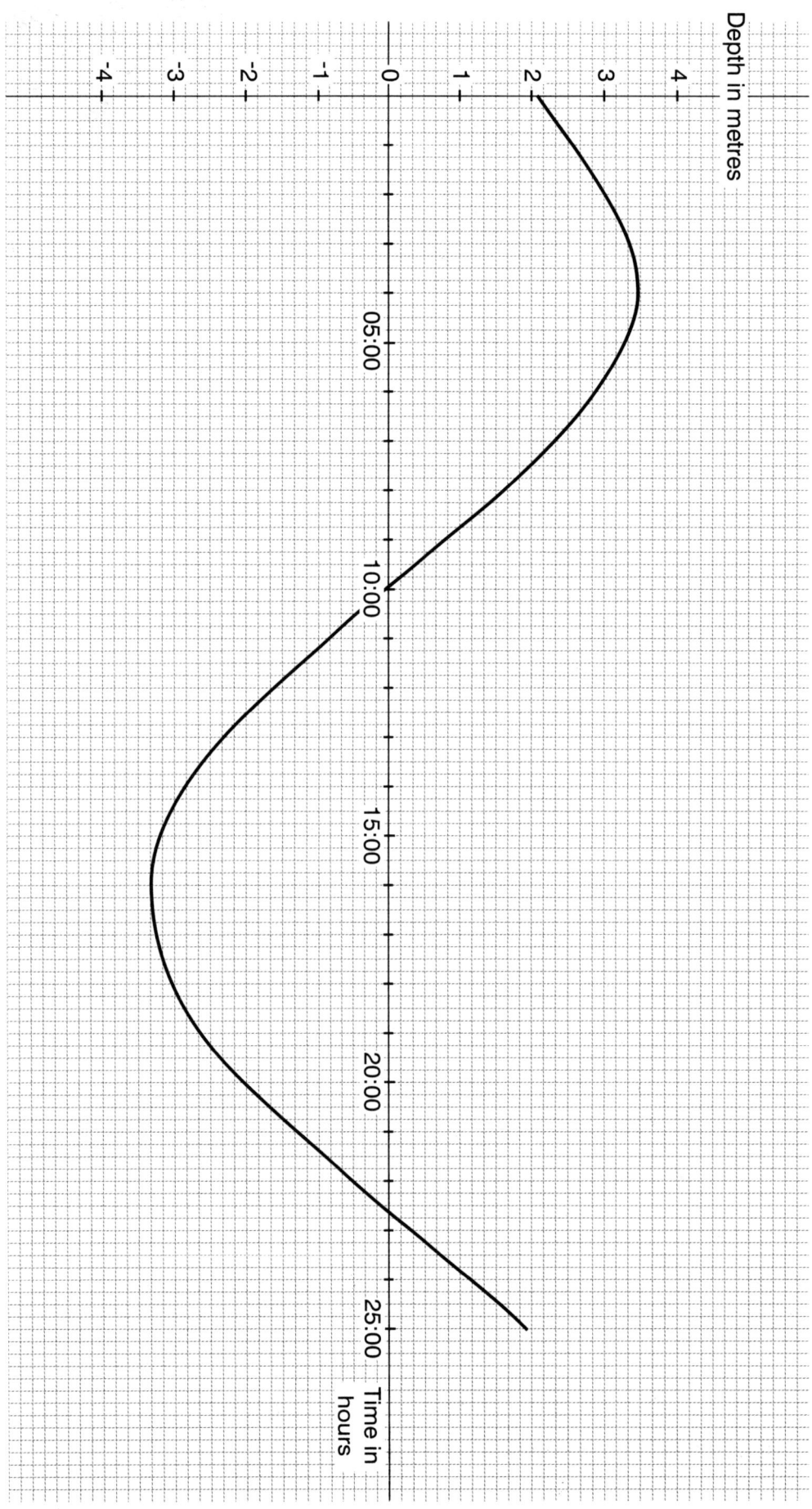

Depth in metres

-4 -3 -2 -1 0 1 2 3 4

05:00 10:00 15:00 20:00 25:00

Time in hours

Graph of height against time for a small 1 tonne oxygen-powered rocket

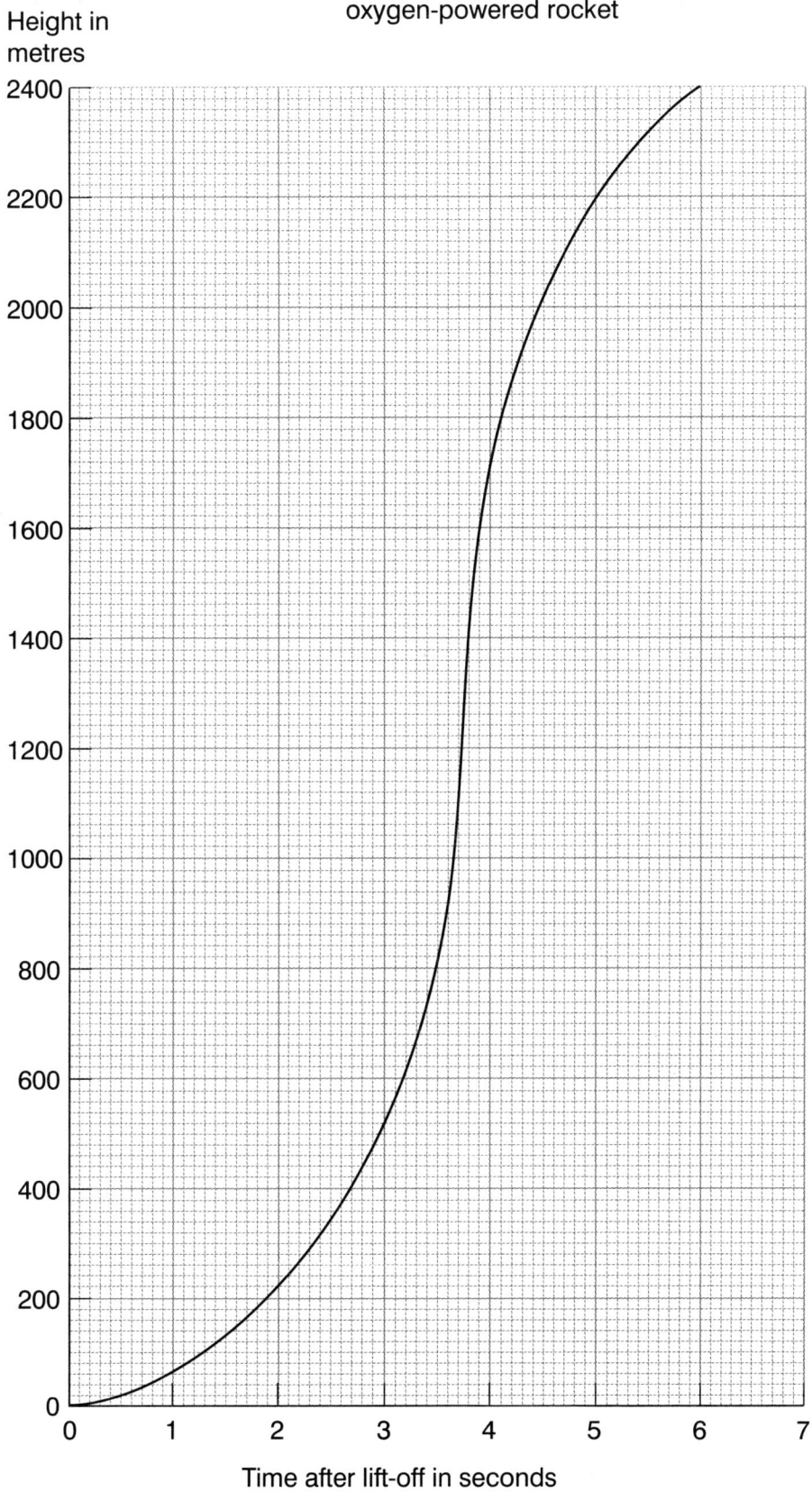

Height in metres (y-axis, 0 to 2400)

Time after lift-off in seconds (x-axis, 0 to 7)

Velocity in
metres per second

Graph of velocity against time for a small
oxygen-powered rocket

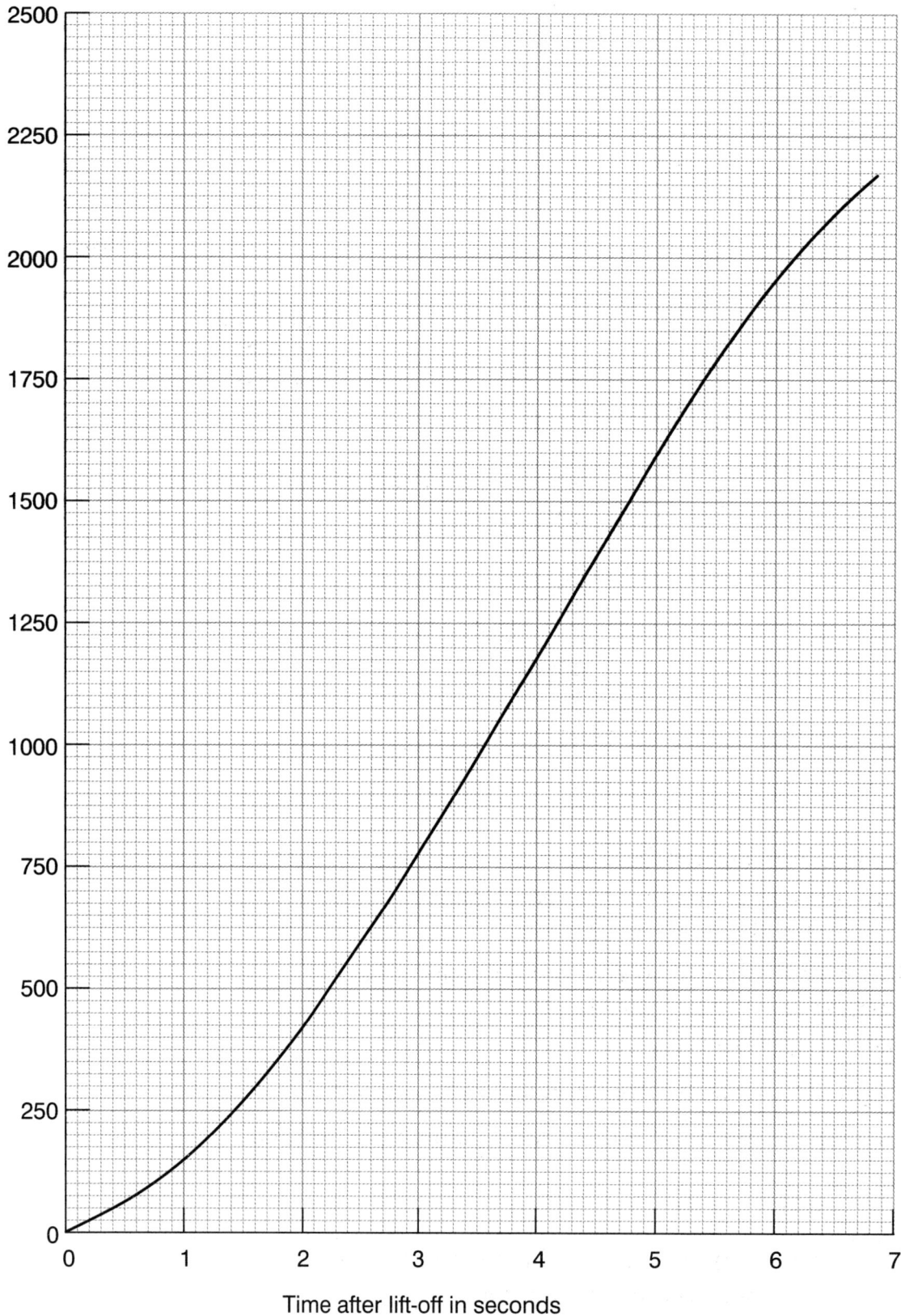

Time after lift-off in seconds

B1 This is a screen dump from a graph-plotting program.
It shows four graphs: y1, y2, y3 and y4.

(a) Match each graph with its equation.

(b) Use the graphs to answer these questions:
   (i) What values of x give $x^2 - x - 2$ a value of zero?
   (ii) Solve the equation $x^2 - x - 2 = 0$.

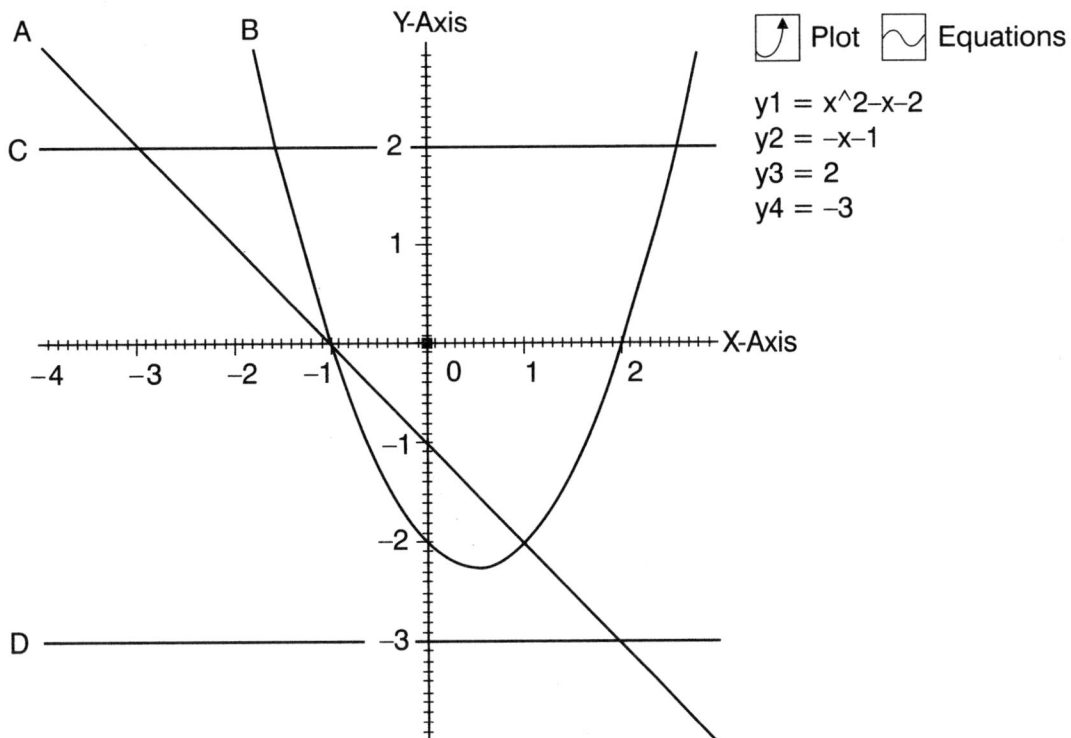

Y-Axis

⤴ Plot 〜 Equations

y1 = x^2–x–2
y2 = –x–1
y3 = 2
y4 = –3

X-Axis

B2 Use the graphs to answer these.

(a) Solve the pair of simultaneous equations
$y = {}^-x - 1$ and $y = x^2 - x - 2$.

(b) Will your answers to (a) give you the roots of the
equation ${}^-x - 1 = x^2 - x - 2$?
Explain your answer.

B3 Use one of the graphs to solve the equation $x^2 - x - 2 = 2$.

B4 Explain why the solutions to these two equations are the same.
$$x^2 - x - 2 = 2$$
$$x^2 - x - 4 = 0$$

B5 How could you convince someone that the equation
$x^2 - x - 2 = {}^-3$ does not have any solutions?

B6 This is another screen dump from a graph-plotting program.
It shows the two graphs $y = x^3$ and $y = 2x^2 + x - 1$.

Use the graphs to solve, correct to one decimal place, these
equations.

(a) $2x^2 + x - 1 = 0$ (b) $x^3 = 2$ (c) $2x^2 + x - 1 = x^3$

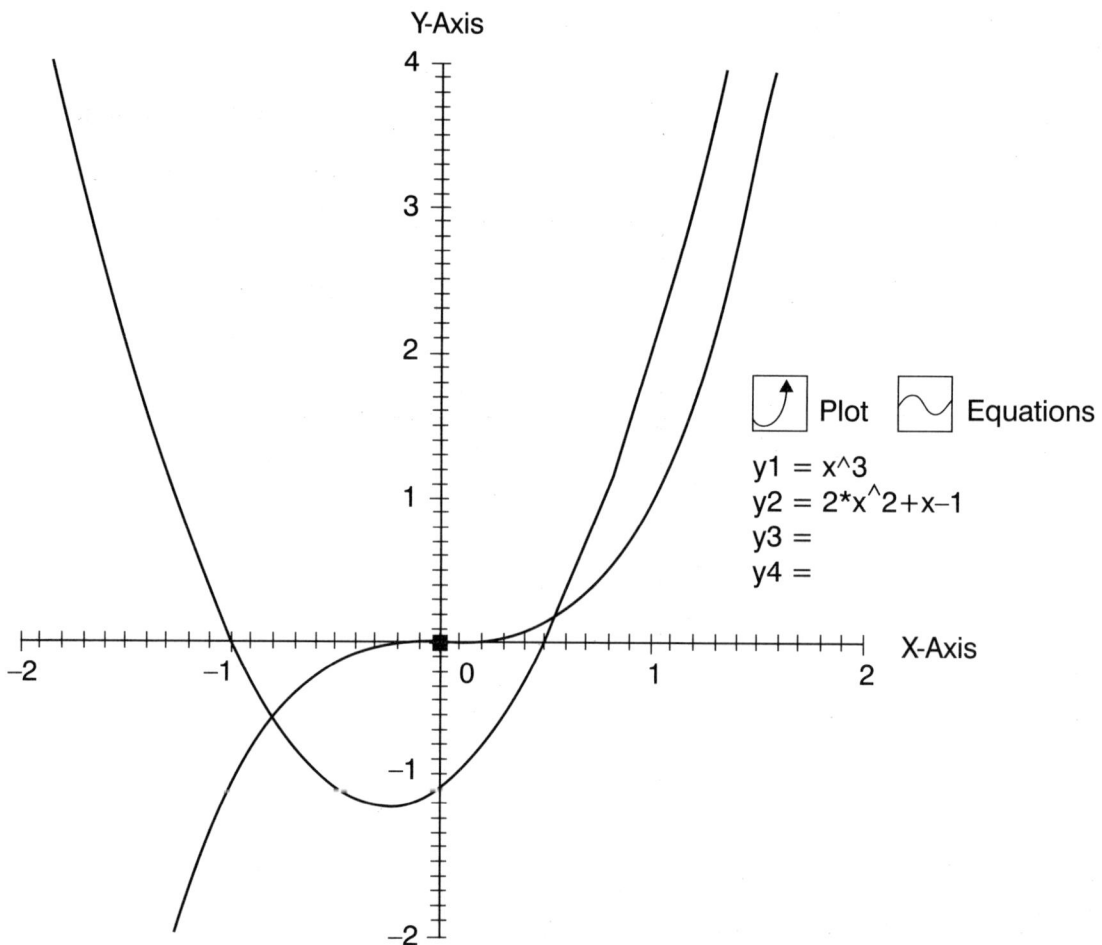

Plot   Equations

y1 = x^3
y2 = 2*x^2+x–1
y3 =
y4 =

B7 Solve these equations to one decimal place. (You may
need to draw in some straight lines.)

(a) $x^3 = x$ (b) $2x^2 - 1 = 0$ (c) $2x^2 + x = 0$

B8 Use a graphical calculator or graph-drawing program for
this question.

Is there a third root to the equation $2x^2 + x - 1 = x^3$?

If there is, give it to the nearest whole number.

B16 Here is a screen dump showing the graphs
$y = 10 \cos x - 10 \sin x$, $y = 5$, $y = 3x$ and $y = {}^-3x$.
The value of x ranges from 0 to 2π.

Use the graphs to help you find the solutions to these
equations to the nearest 0·1 radian.

(a) $10 \cos x - 10 \sin x = 0$ (b) $10 \cos x - 10 \sin x = 5$

(c) $10 \cos x - 10 \sin x = {}^-3x$ (d) $10 \cos x = 10 \sin x + 5$

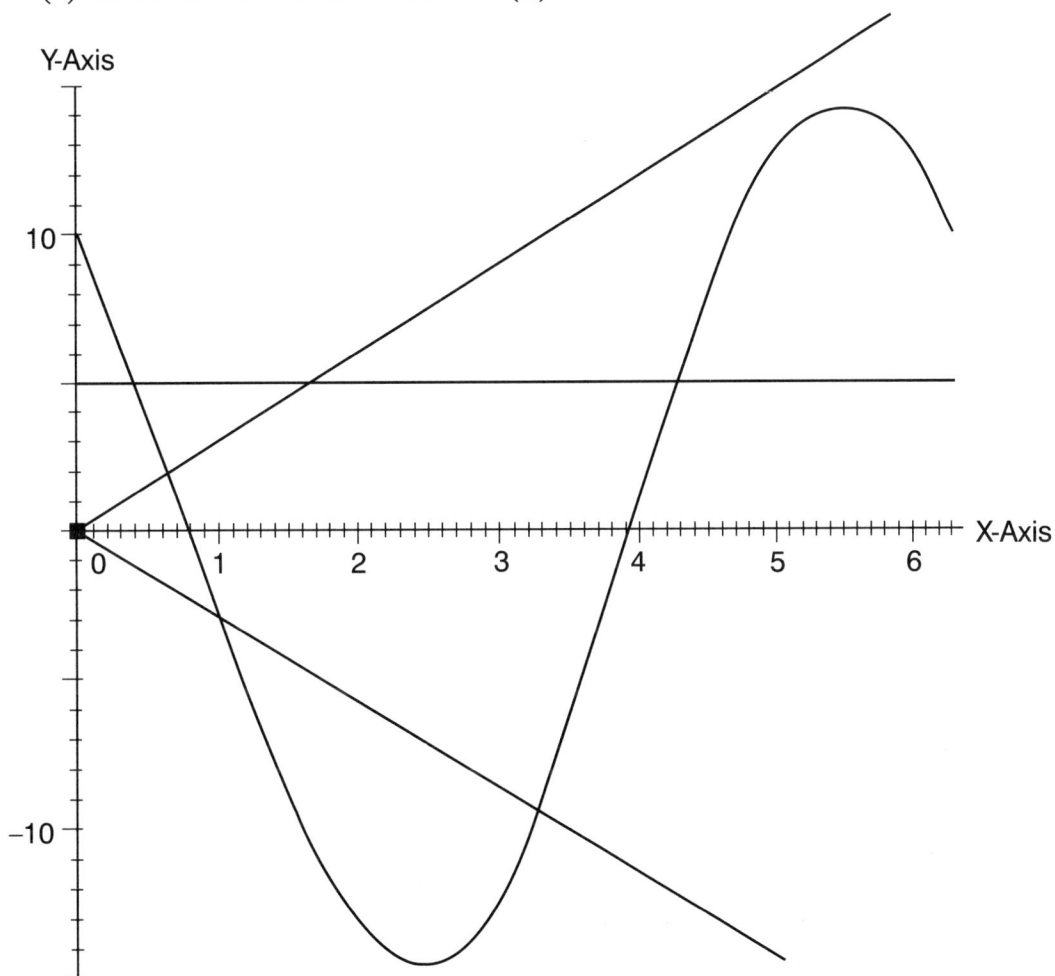

☑ Plot   〰 Equations

y1 = 10*cos (x) –10*sin (x)
y2 = 5
y3 = 3*x
y4 = –3*x

SOLD AS PACK ??   D/6/2000